Contents

Acknowledgements

The author would like to thank the following for technical advice freely given during the preparation of this book: Redland Bricks Ltd., The Brick Development Association, and the Cement and Concrete Association.

Picture credits
All photographs have been taken by the author, except for the following, whom the author and publishers would like to thank for their help: Alton, Banbury Homes and Gardens Ltd p. 74; Brick Development Association p. 46; Cement and Concrete Association p. 16 (both pictures); Stapeley Water Gardens pp. 66 (all pictures), 87.

The publishers would like to thank Kevin Dean for all the line and colour artwork.

A BLANDFORD GARDENING HANDBOOK

Garden Construction

Peter McHoy

BLANDFORD PRESS
POOLE · DORSET

First published in the U.K., 1984 by Blandford Press, Link House, West Street, Poole, Dorset, BH15 1LL.

Copyright © 1984 Blandford Press Ltd.

Distributed in the United States by Sterling Publishing Co., Inc., 2 Park Avenue, New York, N.Y. 10016.

ISBN 0 7137 1245 7 (Hardback)
 0 7137 1416 6 (Paperback)

British Library Cataloguing in Publication Data

McHoy, Peter
  Garden construction.—(A Blandford gardening handbook)
  1. Gardening
  I. Title
  635   SB450.97

Typeset in Hong Kong by Graphicraft Typesetters
Printed in Great Britain by A. Wheaton & Co., Ltd., Exeter

Introduction

Gardening is essentially a practical, active pastime. The creation of the garden is as much a part of the pleasure as the beauty of the plants. If it were finished results alone that held the key to satisfaction, few of us would bother with a garden of our own when there are so many wonderful gardens that we can visit. It is the sense of achievement at creating a garden on our own small plot of land that is part of the reward.

The background of garden features can make the garden as much as any individual plant. The best plants will not guarantee an attractive garden, but a well-constructed framework of garden features can look interesting with quite ordinary plants.

This book cannot be a blueprint for success. The best-made feature can look hideous in the wrong place; you must always consider the overall design of the garden before taking up the spade or the hammer.

Because everything should be adapted to your own needs and garden, the emphasis has been on principles. Nobody can tell you how to build a rock garden stone by stone, as every site is different and no two stones are alike. Neither will you find exact dimensions for a garden seat as it makes little difference if a patio seat is 15 cm (6 in) longer or shorter, and by adapting it to fit exactly you will have something that is just right for your needs.

All the jobs described are within the scope of a handyman with average ability. Some of the earth-moving jobs are hard work, however, and it is no disgrace to hire a little help with these — particularly if you are in a hurry to get things finished. Likewise, removing a tree stump is a simple, routine job to someone with the right mechanical equipment, but a lengthy and exhausting business to do yourself, even if you like a challenge.

The book is arranged in three parts. Part One is all about making a start: how to clear the ground and prepare the site, and tools to make the job easier. Part Two deals with actual construction: how to make many different garden features from a flower bed to a patio, as well as general advice on aspects such as erecting a greenhouse or installing an outside water supply. Part Three is a guide to shopping for materials, and should take some of the mystique out of buying things like bricks and mortar, as well as plants.

Many garden construction jobs that seem formidable at first are simple if you tackle them step by step. I hope that this book will give you that extra confidence to encourage you to make a start.

Making a Start

No matter how well you plan your garden on paper, or how clearly you see it in the mind's eye, there comes a point at which the dream has to be translated into reality. Reality comes home with impact when you are confronted by a neglected garden, or a rubble-strewn building plot. The prospect can seem no less daunting if you are planning a major redesign of an established garden.

The problem lies mostly in the mind. It is rather like taking a dip in the sea — the first step can be formidable, yet once you are in it is exciting and invigorating. Once you have moved the first few shovelfuls of soil, and can see that you have made *some* impact, the prospect seems challenging rather than daunting.

As in all things, foundations are important, and clearing and preparing the site methodically and thoroughly is the first step towards a good foundation for building a better garden. Sometimes it involves major earth-moving and other heavy work, but the right tools and techniques will make the task easier (do not forget that many of the tools can be hired), and of course you can always hire a little help if you are not up to the heavier tasks. All that matters is that the work is done thoroughly.

You can make a start on your garden at almost any time of the year. Winter is a good time to clear rough ground or to level and prepare an area that you are going to make into a lawn. If you do this in plenty of time, the ground will have time to settle and you can hoe off any weed seedlings that germinate before you sow or turf. If you have just moved into an established garden, however, it may be worth waiting for a few months to see whether any useful plants come up that are worth saving.

1 Site Preparation

Clearing the Ground

If the ground is at all rough, clear the site first. Collect any rubble into heaps (you might need it for hardcore), and remove any shrubs, hedges or trees that have to be cleared. Never remove any of these, however, unless you have given the matter careful thought at the planning stage. Remember also to be particularly careful about bringing down any old trees that might have a preservation order on them.

Removing a large tree is not a job for the amateur; but it is worth getting several quotes from reputable firms (you will find tree surgeons listed in your classified telephone directory). Make sure that the company is fully insured. If you want to tackle a small tree yourself, it is worth hiring a chain saw, but remember that chain saws can be very dangerous in inexperienced hands, so wear goggles, sensible clothes and boots, and use common sense. If you are doing more than a few minutes' work, wear ear muffs. You can also hire winches, which are useful for removing small stumps. A large stump is best dealt with by a contractor, who will grind it out if it cannot be pulled out.

When obstacles have been removed, an overgrown or neglected garden may still need clearing of plant growth before detailed marking-out can begin. Avoid the temptation to use long-lasting weed-killers such as sodium chlorate or simazine (even if you have plenty of time before you expect to start planting). If it is just the top growth that you want to clear, paraquat will do the job admirably and the ground will be perfectly safe for planting when you are ready. If there are many deep-rooted perennials that you ought to clear at the same time, try one based on glyphosate; it will kill off most plants but the ground will soon be safe for planting. If you have a flame gun, you can use this of course, though tough perennials will come up again.

There is no point in digging over areas that are to be paved (but it is still best to clear the weeds), and even sections that are to be cultivated are best left undug until you have marked out the garden and are ready to tackle that section. Walking over freshly dug or cultivated soil while working is not only very dusty or muddy (depending on the weather), but it is also very difficult to wheel barrows.

When individual areas have to be prepared for planting you can hand dig if the area is small, but for a large area you will find it useful to hire a rotary cultivator.

It is particularly important to prepare the ground thoroughly for lawns, trees and shrubs. These will be in position for a long time and it is not easy to rectify short cuts made at this stage.

Levelling

Reasonably accurate levelling is vital not only for laying a lawn or a paved area (you may want a slight slope on these, but it ought to be controlled), but also for the general appearance of the garden.

Tackle the job methodically, otherwise you will do a lot of needless shovelling and barrowing of soil, and possibly end up burying the good top-soil with undesirable sub-soil.

If it is only a matter of levelling uneven ground, it may be sufficient to achieve the desired results without any need for digging; but do not trust your eye unless it is in an area that really does not matter. It is simple to use pegs, a straight-edge and a spirit-level (*see* below).

If the level has to be changed substantially, remove the top-soil and stack it on one side. Remove the sub-soil to the required level, then return the top-soil. Obviously this is a heavy job to tackle on any scale, and you may wish to consider the alternative of buying in some good top-soil (look in the classified section of your local newspaper), to bring up the level of the lower part. This will not always be possible if the design calls for a lowering rather than a raising of level.

Before you level any area, always consider the plan as a whole: the surplus from one area can sometimes be used elsewhere, and carting it straight there in the first place will save a lot of needless handling.

Ground that can appear level at first glance may really need levelling. Pegs and spirit-level can be revealing!

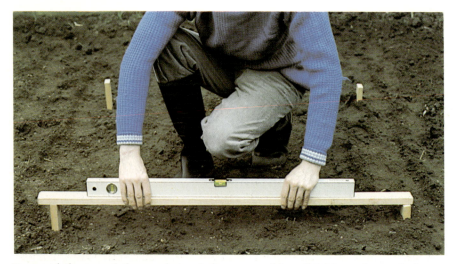

To avoid the top of the peg being below ground in a 'high' patch, mark the pegs about 25 mm (1 in) from the top.

Level the ground to the mark on the pegs. If the ground is not too uneven you should be able to do this with a rake.

Changing Level

If you have drawn up your garden plan with thought, the chances are that you have tried to introduce changes of level rather than attempted to reduce the site to a flat common denominator.

If the site is naturally sloping, but the changes in level are not great, it is simple to lay a course of bricks or stone to form a transition between one level and another, or to use steps, with a small bank if necessary, to link the beds or lawn areas. An earth bank will not look odd once planted with suitable shrubs or ground-cover plants.

Sometimes the problem is one of creating a change of height in what is an otherwise flat site. The easiest process for producing natural contours is the reverse of the cut-and-fill method of levelling. Simply by lowering the ground immediately in front of the raised area, a greater impression of height can be gained with the minimum of earth-moving. Remember, however, not to bury the top-soil. You will find it easiest to barrow the soil up a slope by using a stout plank.

A steep bank will require a retaining wall, complete with drainage escape holes if it is large.

If you have a sloping site, it may be best to make the change of level a positive one.

Drainage

If you are not sure whether it is worth laying drains, take out holes 30 cm (1 ft) deep at various points in the garden shortly after heavy rain. If a quantity of water seeps into the bottom of the hole after a few hours, the land will probably benefit from improved drainage.

Of course if you have planned a bog garden you can take advantage of the high water table, and even feed the land drains into this direction. Generally, however, you must choose the site for a soakaway carefully and it should be at least 1.2 m (4 ft) deep, with 90 cm (3 ft) of rubble at the bottom. This ought to be covered with a thick layer of gravel, and if you prefer it the whole sump can be topped with turf.

As the drains should be laid with a slight fall, the soakaway should naturally be constructed at a low point in the garden, but *not* near the house.

You can buy land drains from a good builder's merchant, and you should also be able to buy the tiles to cover them from the same source.

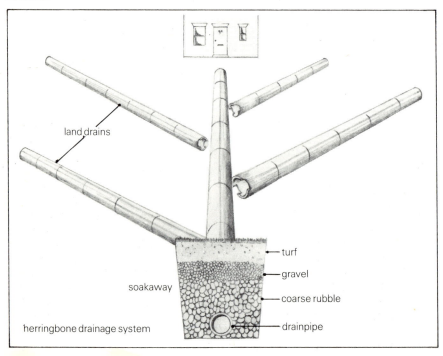

land drains

turf

gravel

soakaway

coarse rubble

herringbone drainage system

drainpipe

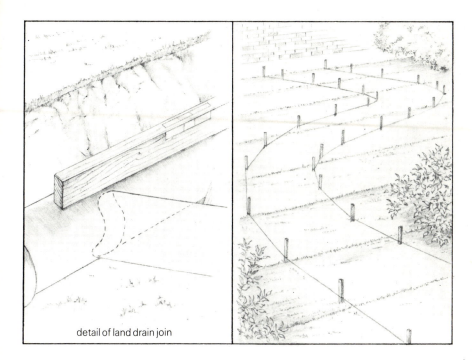

detail of land drain join

Marking-out

If you are to save a lot of wasted effort, and you want the garden to look well designed, it is always best to work from a plan (see *Garden Planning and Design*, in this series).

Start by marking out the major areas: lawn, patio, vegetable plot, and any sections involving a change of level. This should enable you to deal with the major tasks of levelling, and any changes of level.

Nothing more elaborate is needed than strong pegs (best painted white) and a few balls of strong string. You do not need to worry if it is a centimetre or two out for the initial site clearance and preparation.

Paved areas, including paths, and walls must be pegged out accurately, and steps need special care, but flowing borders have a little more flexibility. It is easier to sow or lay your lawn as a rectangle first, and cut beds and borders into it later. A length of hosepipe can be used as a guide between known points if you want to produce a curved edge to a lawn, but formal beds in a lawn need careful and accurate measuring — the techniques are described on page 28.

2 Tools

There is an expression that it is a bad workman that blames his tools, but there is no doubt that the right tools make a job both easier and quicker. Most of the equipment required for garden construction are basic garden and DIY household tools anyway, but there are a few specialized items that are worth buying or hiring.

If you have a lot of construction to tackle, and you do not already have a good quality spade, fork and rake, it is worth considering some of the professional tools (normally available from a good builder's

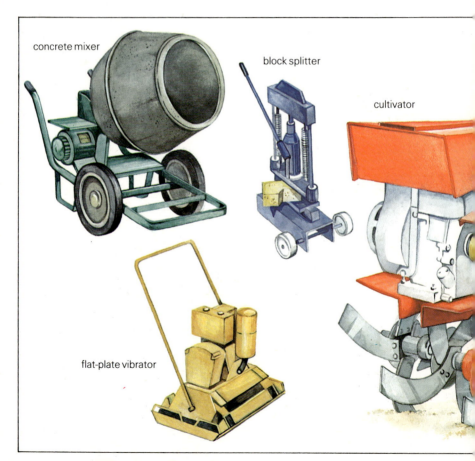

concrete mixer

block splitter

cultivator

flat-plate vibrator

merchant), which are strong and made for this sort of work. On the other hand, if you have *quality* tools already you will be able to manage quite well with those.

A pickaxe or a mattock are often surprisingly useful, while a crowbar or 'jemmy' will come in handy. These can be hired.

A good wheelbarrow is essential. There are many designs, most perfectly adequate for normal garden use, but for construction work you need a strong one, preferably with a pneumatic tyre. On the other hand, avoid one that is so heavy that it tests your muscles even when empty; professional builders are accustomed to such muscular work, most part-timers are not.

garden roller

chain saw

Left: ready-mixed concrete will save you a lot of time and effort, but you must have suitable access, and everything will have to be prepared ready to receive it.

Below: If you mix concrete yourself, save time and effort by arranging the mixer and materials to cut down wasted motion.

It is sensible to wear gloves for this sort of work. They will save a lot of knocks (and curses) when you are handling paving slabs, mixing cement, and the like. Obviously they should be strong. They will come in useful long after the garden has been constructed.

If you are going to lay paving or bricks, you will need a bolster (a special kind of chisel with a broad blade for cutting paving) and a lump hammer (it has a short handle and a heavy head of about 1-2 kg or 2-4 lb). A builder's trowel will be needed for placing mortar, and the bigger it is the better (once you get used to handling a large one). All these items are worth buying as they are useful tools to have around the home.

A good spirit-level is also a wise investment, and you will use it a lot in garden construction for levelling ground as well as laying paving or bricks. It ought to be 60 or 90 cm (2 or 3 ft) long; do not try to make do with some pocket version if you can afford a large one. If you have to use a small one, fix it to an absolutely straight and true piece of timber about 90 cm (3 ft) long.

A wooden square can be useful, and easy to make yourself. You can use two pieces of 50 × 25 mm (2 × 1 in) or 75 × 25 mm (3 × 1 in) prepared timber to form a right-angled 'L' (use a try-square to test for accuracy), joining with a screwed and glued halved joint. A third piece of timber should be screwed at a 45° angle to give rigidity (*see* page 41).

Alternatively you can ensure that your right-angles are correct by using string. The method is described here as it is applicable to many jobs described later in the book. Stretch a taut line along your known straight line, then tie a 90 cm (3 ft) length of string to a peg at the corner point, and a 1.5 m (5 ft) length 1.2 m (4 ft) from the corner. Pull them both taut and drive a peg in where they meet. It is not so accurate but is adequate for many jobs.

If you are mixing concrete, you might want to consider hiring a mixer; there are some electrically-driven models that are adequate for small quantities. If you are laying a large area of concrete for paths or foundations, you may want to consider having it delivered ready mixed, if you have suitable access, but for most garden jobs it is easier to mix it as you require it — then you can work at your own pace.

If you are going to erect fences and gates, the hardest job is getting the posts in correctly, and here the right tools can make all the difference. A post borer is worth hiring if you have many post-holes to prepare. Failing that, a large iron bar about 1.2 m (4 ft) long is useful for opening up holes.

A saw and carpenter's claw hammer are obviously useful.

Construction

There is a temptation to rush at the various garden features to be constructed, in the urge to see finished results. The kind of exhibition gardens you see erected at some of the famous shows within a matter of days are put up by a team of experts with plenty of back-up, and as they are only erecting something that has to last a week rather than a lifetime they can take short-cuts.

For the gardener doing it in his spare time, as a *pleasurable* exercise, it is entirely different. It does not really matter if it takes you a year or more to finish the job, and spreading the tasks over a period not only evens the workload but also avoids heavy expenditure all at once.

On the other hand it is important to see progress, otherwise interest is likely to flag. The answer is to construct one feature at a time, and *finish* that. Then go on to the next job. If you deal with some of the major jobs first, such as paving, fencing (or hedges), and the lawn, you will have the framework for the rest of the garden, which can be tackled later. It is worth giving priority to trees and shrubs too, so that these can be getting established with the least delay. Pergolas, garden seats and raised beds can all be tackled later while the framework plants are becoming established.

One way of emphasizing a change of level to make it more positive is to lower the ground just in front of the retaining wall, rather like a ha-ha. It looks very natural and permanent in a mature setting, but someone once had the job of constructing this.

3 Making a Lawn

The lawn is a central feature in most gardens, so it deserves special thought and care in laying or sowing.

The decision of whether to sow seed or lay turf is largely a question of use and cost. For rough use, coarse grasses may be perfectly adequate, and in certain settings there is nothing wrong with a few lawn weeds. Turf will usually provide a satisfactory lawn quickly, and you can actually buy turf prepared from sown grasses as opposed to meadow turf. For a quality lawn, or an inexpensive coarser lawn, however, sowing is the answer.

Regardless of the type of grass you are sowing, thorough ground preparation is essential if you want a trouble-free lawn later. Nothing looks less professional than a lawn with 'hills and vales'. Although mowing and modern selective weedkillers will quickly put paid to most weeds there is no point in starting at a disadvantage, and in the early months weeds will compete for nutrients and light at the very time the grass is trying to become established.

If the ground is likely to become waterlogged, lay drains (*see* page 12), and in any case fork over the ground to remove as many perennial weed roots as possible. Be particularly careful to remove coarse grass roots, as you will not be able to remove these with selective weedkillers once the lawn is established.

Rake the ground level, checking with the method described on page 9 if necessary. Then tread the whole area to consolidate the ground, and use a roller if you have one (but the ground should be dry for these operations). It is best to do this some weeks before laying or sowing. Any weed seedlings that appear in the meantime should be hoed off.

If the ground is poor or the soil very light, or very heavy, and you are going to sow seed, work in as much damp peat as you can spare into the top 7.5 cm (3 in). This is not necessary for turf. A week before sowing or laying, poor soil will benefit from an *autumn* lawn feed (summer feeds will have too much nitrogen, but autumn feeds contain more phosphates, for root growth).

A Lawn from Seed

A lawn will only be as good as the seed you sow. Most seed companies offer a range of mixtures from the very finest to coarse, hard-wearing types that will take a lot of punishment but not look so good. Nevertheless there are many strains, and it pays to buy from a seedsman with a reputation for good grass seed. It is now possible to buy a strain of hard-wearing ryegrass that makes a very compact, slow-growing plant. This means a better quality hard-wearing lawn and less mowing.

Special shade mixtures are available, but do not expect any grass to make a fine lawn beneath trees.

The *rate* of sowing depends very much on the type of grasses the mixture contains and is usually in the range of 35–70 g per m² (1–2 oz per sq yd). Be guided by the recommendation on the packet; some mixtures contain many very fine seeds, whereas others contain fewer but larger seeds, so with some you will sow more seeds in a given area by sowing at half the rate of another kind. There is no point in sowing extra — it is just a waste of money; the sowing rates even allow for the birds taking a few seeds, although it is often treated to make it unpalatable.

Sow evenly. The best way is to sow half working across the ground in one direction, then the other half working across at right angles to the first application. Never apply it by shaking through a sieve, as this will separate out the various types of grass in a mixture. You can mark out the ground into square metres or yards, but for a large area you will find it much easier just to mark 1 metre (yard) intervals along opposite sides, measure enough for the strip, and work in this way. If you do it in two halves as suggested you will achieve an even cover with the minimum of effort.

Lightly rake it in. You can give it a light rolling if you have a roller, but this is not essential. The seed should not be buried deeper than 6 mm ($\frac{1}{4}$ in), otherwise germination will be affected.

Even if the seed has been treated to make it unpalatable, it is worth using bird scarers, as they will still be attracted by the sight of the seed. A few strands of black cotton stretched across is usually adequate to stop birds taking dust-baths if the ground is dryish.

Bird scarers lose their effectiveness if left in one position. Use several kinds, different ones on different days, and move them about.

The best time to sow is spring or early autumn (preferably September). The soil should be warm and damp. You can sow throughout the summer, but regular irrigation will be essential.

In any case, always keep the ground well watered, preferably with a fine sprinkler, until the seed has germinated and is growing well.

Wait until the grass is about 7.5 cm (3 in) high before attempting to cut it, and then keep the mower blade sharp and high. Do not take more than 2.5 cm (1 in) off for the first few cuts.

Rather than attempting to sow curves and sweeps, it is better to keep

Before sowing lawn seed, rake the ground thoroughly.

Tread the soil firmly to settle it, then rake again.

Mark off in metre or yard strips and sow evenly.

Rake the seed in lightly, removing footmarks as you go.

to straight lines at first, then cut into the grass once it becomes established. In this way you should have nice clean edges with grass growing strongly right to the edge.

Pre-seeded Rolls

If you fancy a lawn that you simply unroll and cut to shape with scissors, then pre-seeded rolls might appeal. The seeds are embedded in a biodegradable base. The roll usually has to be soaked for a few days before laying, and is then simply unrolled on to a prepared bed. Cover with a fine layer of soil, preferably sieved, and water it daily if the weather is dry. It is obviously more expensive than sowing loose seed, but you do get an even cover, there is less chance of birds being a problem, and there is some degree of weed suppression (though you must expect some weeds in all newly-sown lawns). You must still prepare the ground properly.

A grass roll is simply cut to size with scissors.

Each strip must be covered with a layer of fine soil.

A Lawn from Turf

Turf takes more physical effort and time to lay (although ground preparation need not be quite so thorough), but you do have an instant lawn.

Although turf can be laid throughout the summer if you water thoroughly until established, the best time is September to early March, provided that the soil is not frozen or waterlogged.

One of the difficulties of turf is the variable quality. Because of carriage costs, it is usually necessary to rely mainly on local sources of supply, which are often no more than reasonably weed-free meadow grass. Often this is perfectly adequate for a general-purpose lawn, but it still pays to inspect the turf before buying if at all possible (not always easy).

There are specialist growers who raise turf from particular seed mixtures, and these can be of a very high standard. Naturally they are more expensive, but if you want a good ornamental lawn from turf it is worth paying the extra.

Turf should be laid within a couple of days of delivery. If the weather prevents this, unroll each piece in a shady place and keep watered. Follow the step-by-step instructions below and opposite.

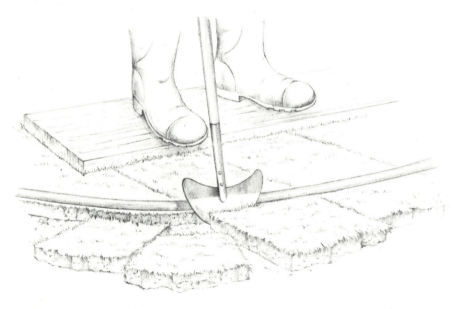

Above: Stagger the joins when you lay turf, and if you have to stand on the newly-laid grass use a plank of wood to distribute your weight.

Right: You can make yourself a 'turf beater' out of a slightly wedge-shaped piece of wood. Use it to firm down each newly laid turf (it is better than banging it down with the back of a spade!).

Left: It is best to lay your turf in rectangles, and cut out shapes afterwards.

4 Making Flower Beds

Borders are usually straightforward to mark out and prepare. Straight-edged borders normally run parallel to a fence or path, so it is simply a matter of measuring off from there; you can use a square to check that the right-angles are true.

Curved borders are a little trickier but easily marked out if the narrow and wide points are measured off from a known point (perhaps a fence or path), and something flexible such as a hosepipe used to link these points in graceful curves. Use an edging iron or sand to transfer the outline of the curve.

If a bed falls in an isolated area with no easy reference points to measure from, you can transfer the positions from your plan by triangulation. This may be useful for pinpointing the position of a bed for a specimen tree, although you can often judge something like this by eye.

To find a position by triangulation, measure off the distance on your scale plan from two convenient points (*see* below); where arcs from these points meet is the position you require.

It is the formal, geometric type of layout that causes the most problems; often the beds must be symmetrical and carefully positioned so that they balance an overall design.

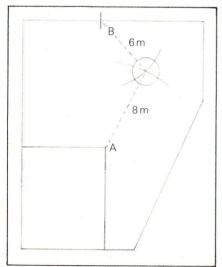

Positioning a bed from your plan can often be done by eye, but if you want to be precise you can use the method shown on the left. Simply measure off from two known points on your plan, and where the two lines intersect is the position you want.

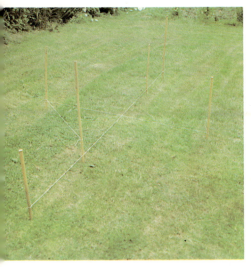

Above left and right: Marking out an oval is not as difficult as it looks, and you will probably find it easier to do than to read about. The method is described on the next page.

Right: use a half-moon edger, not a spade, to provide a neat edge to a bed (a spade is slightly curved and will not produce a straight line). A suitable piece of wood will help to keep the line on course.

A circular bed is easy to construct. Drive a strong stake into the central position, slip a piece of string with a loop on the end over the stake, and keeping the string taut scribe a circle with another stick attached to the other end. The string should be the radius (half the width) of the final bed, and the loop should revolve freely round the central stake, so that it does not have a 'winding up' effect.

An oval is much more difficult. First place pegs at the top, bottom and two widest points of the oval. Attaching a string to the top and bottom pegs and one between the two side pegs will enable you to determine that you have them placed centrally (they should form a cross, with an equal amount of string either side of the intersection with the other string). Next attach a piece of string *half the length* of the oval, to one of the *side* pegs and stretch it across so that it intersects the longest piece of string. Insert a peg, then stretch it towards the opposite end and insert another peg where it intersects. You now have six pegs (*see* illustrations on pages 27 and 29).

Cut a piece of string twice the length between one of these inner pegs on the long string and the peg farthest away. Form it into a loop, and drape it loosely over the inner pegs. Finally, slip a pointed peg within the loop, and keeping it taut scribe an oval as you work round the shape, keeping the string in tension. A sprinkling of sand can be used to emphasize the outline.

If you want an oval where the dimensions do not have to be too exact, you can take a short cut by just inserting two pegs at roughly the position shown for the inner pegs opposite and experimenting with the size of the loop of string and positioning of the pegs until you strike the right combination.

If you fancy an octagonal bed, this is quite simple to achieve. Start by marking out a square, then using a peg in each corner stretch a piece of string to the centre of the square and scribe an arc to the edges of the square. Place a peg where the arc intersects the edge. This will give you the eight points of the octagon.

You can indulge in more complicated shapes, but they will probably look 'fussy', and remember that you will have to mow round them!

Use an edging iron (also known as a half-moon edger) to cut straight edges. The blade of a spade has a slight curve and it is more difficult to achieve a neat, straight edge.

To give the beds a finished look, try to ensure that there is a reasonably deep edge to the bed, with the soil gradually mounded towards the middle of the bed.

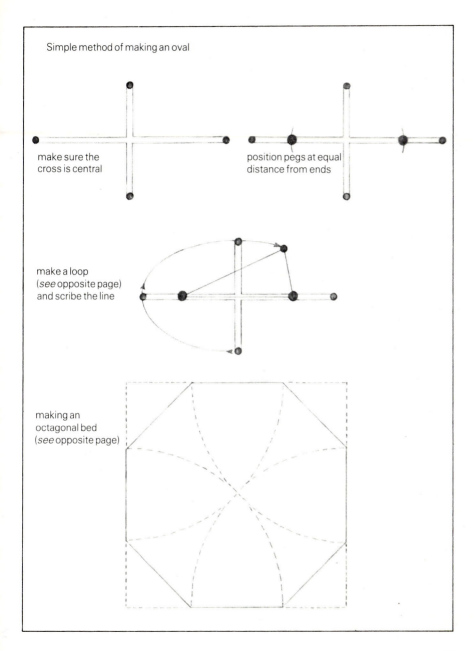

Simple method of making an oval

make sure the cross is central

position pegs at equal distance from ends

make a loop (*see* opposite page) and scribe the line

making an octagonal bed (*see* opposite page)

5 Erecting a Fence

Fences are not cheap (perhaps twice the price of many hedges) but they are likely to be only half the price of a brick or screen (pierced concrete) block wall. You do have instant privacy, and a useful background against which to train many plants.

Most gardeners choose wooden fencing, though metal or plastic fences are available. Chain link fencing, often plastic-coated, is reasonably priced, and is worth considering where you need to keep animals in (or out) without obscuring a good view.

As privacy is often an important consideration, 'solid' wooden fences are the ones usually erected.

Types of Fence

Close-board (or feathered) fences can be erected on site, but it is more usual to buy panels. The vertical boards are tapered ('feathered') on the edge that overlaps. They form a good screen, but even so gaps can appear as the wood shrinks with age.

Interwoven fences have a decorative finish to the panels, but are not usually 'peep-proof'.

Overlap fences have horizontally overlapping boards. They provide good privacy.

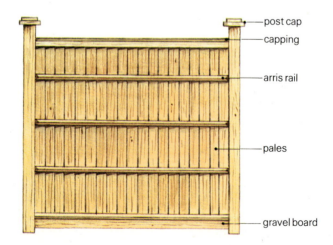

post cap

capping

arris rail

pales

gravel board

interwoven   trellis   wattle hurdle

overlap   closeboard   post and rail

Picket (or palisade) fences are most in keeping with cottage gardens, and are usually painted.

Post and rail fences (there are wooden and plastic versions) are useful in rural settings where the minimum obstruction of view is required, but obviously they do not form much of a barrier.

The first three mentioned are all erected as described and illustrated on pp. 32-3. For picket and post and rail fences, the basic principles of preparing secure posts and ensuring that the fence is true vertically and horizontally remain the same.

Erecting a Timber Fence

Start by clearing the ground and stretching a garden line where the fence is to be erected, to give you an accurate line to work to.

The most difficult part of erecting a fence is digging the post-holes, and making sure that the posts are securely fixed in the correct position.

Dig your post-holes perhaps a little over 30 cm (1 ft) wide at the top, tapering to 23 cm (9 in) at the bottom, and about 60 cm (2 ft) deep. You might find it less effort to hire a post-hole borer if the soil is not too stony. Bricks and large stones have to be tackled with a crowbar.

Calculate the distance required between holes; most panels are 1.8 m (6 ft) long, and posts 7.5 cm (3 in) across. These measurements added together give you the distance from the centre-point of one hole to the next.

Mix enough concrete (6 parts combined aggregate to 1 part cement) for two or three post-holes (allow 50 kg [1 cwt] per hole).

Insert the first post, having first sawn off any excess if necessary, and use the spirit-level to check verticals, wedging it with stones if

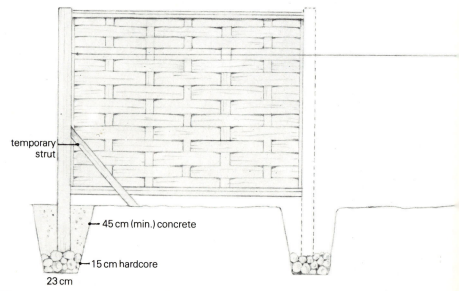

temporary strut

45 cm (min.) concrete

15 cm hardcore

23 cm

necessary. Ram the concrete round the bottom 45 cm (1½ ft), then recheck alignment with the spirit-level.

Fix a line to the post at about 90 cm (3 ft) from the ground, and attach the other end to a temporary stake at the other end at the same height. Pull the line taut (use pieces of wood as temporary struts to avoid the post being pulled out of true with the tension).

Recheck adjustment of the first post, then tack the first panel to it, using galvanized nails (ordinary nails will rust), and wedging the other end with a piece of wood if necessary.

Insert the second post, firming it against the first panel, then ram concrete round the base. Check with the spirit-level, including the panel. Tack the panel to the second post.

Repeat until the fence is complete. Then go along nailing the panels firmly, and re-ramming the concrete if necessary. Keep using the spirit-level as you work.

Wedge temporary props along the fence, especially against the posts, to keep everything in position until the concrete has set.

Finish off the posts with post caps.

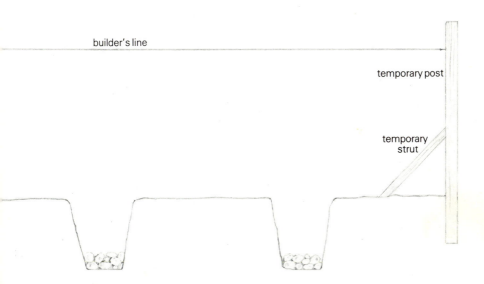

builder's line

temporary post

temporary
strut

Post Supports

There is an excellent alternative to making holes and filling them with concrete. You can buy metal spikes to drive into the ground that will hold most posts securely. You are also assured that the post will not rot off at ground level.

The post support is hammered into the ground with a wooden mallet or a sledge hammer. You need a block of wood to drop into the socket while you are knocking it in (some retailers will hire or loan you a metal device to use). The only difficulty might be in driving it in straight (use a spirit-level as you progress), but a pilot hole made with an iron bar should help.

These post supports are not expensive when you consider that you will save the cost of 60 cm (2 ft) on each support post, and you will not have the cost of the concrete. They are also quick and easy to use.

Preservatives

Always have the wood treated (unless it is heartwood oak or Western red cedar, although even then treatment is beneficial). Creosote is often used, but remember that fresh creosote is lethal to plants. Most organic solvent types, and those applied at the factory under pressure, are safe.

The Legal Aspects

If you are replacing an existing fence, the problem of ownership and responsibility sometimes arises; you cannot always go by which side of the fence the posts are on (they are often on the owner's side, but not invariably). If you are in doubt, the deeds of your property will resolve the matter (these may be with a building society, of course). Naturally it always pays to consult your neighbour anyway.

In Great Britain, you will not need planning permission unless the fence is more than 2 m high (1 m fronting a road), but there may be restrictions placed on you in the deeds, and this is especially likely on 'open plan' housing estates.

In addition, if you erect any fence so high that it will obstruct the view for road users at a dangerous point, you can be made to remove the obstruction.

Fencing is often used in small modern gardens instead of a hedge. A larch-lap fence like this can be quite attractive.

6 Hanging a Gate

Hanging a gate calls for precision, but otherwise it is not a difficult task. Concentration is the key word.

There should be 7.5 cm (3 in) clearance between the ground and the bottom of the gate when closed. Pieces of wood of this thickness are useful as wedges while hanging the gate.

Careful measuring is essential. The space between the two posts should be the width of the gate plus 4 cm ($1\frac{1}{2}$ in) on each side of a single gate. For double gates you will need to allow 4 cm ($1\frac{1}{2}$ in) between each gate and post, with 13 mm ($\frac{1}{2}$ in) in the middle between the two gates, or 20 mm ($\frac{3}{4}$ in) in the case of wooden gates to allow for a little swelling or shrinking.

On metal gates the hinge fittings are normally an integral part of the gate.

On wooden gates you may have to buy gate brackets and hinges if these are not supplied. Gate brackets should be spaced evenly on the edge of the gate. After marking the position of the bolt holes, drill out the holes, then bolt on the brackets. Calculate the position where the hinge fittings are to go on the wooden posts (allowing for a 7.5 cm [3 in] clearance beneath the gate). The bottom fitting is pointed and can be driven into the wood after first taking out a slightly smaller diameter hole with a drill, a few centimetres deep. Be careful to drive it in absolutely straight. The top hinge fitting will probably have a screw thread on it, and a nut which is tightened up after having drilled out a hole slightly smaller in diameter and hammered the spike through.

Concrete posts usually have pre-drilled holes. If these are not suitable, bolt lengths of wood to them and screw hinge fittings to these.

The post itself should be 75 cm ($2\frac{1}{2}$ ft) in the ground, more if the gate is 1.5 m (5 ft) or over.

Pack moist concrete around and beneath the post to achieve the right position (use a spirit-level as well as the tape measure). Apply half the concrete at first; you can top up the rest of the hole once you are satisfied that the gate is correctly hung, with the right clearances.

Support the gate and posts with props and try to leave it for a few days to allow the concrete to set firmly.

There are various gate fittings that you can buy, some suitable for wooden gates, others designed for metal gates. Most bought gates will already have fittings that will dictate the method of hanging.

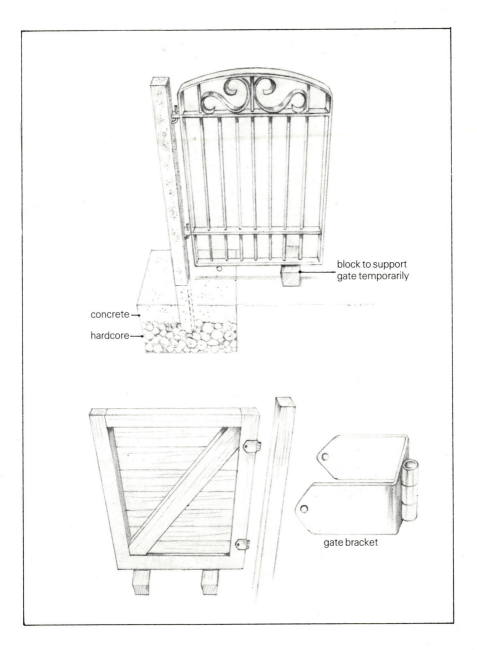

block to support
gate temporarily

concrete

hardcore

gate bracket

7 Building a Wall

Building a boundary wall is more expensive than erecting a fence, and much more expensive than a hedge of the same height. It is, however, permanent and maintenance-free.

Most garden walls built today in fact tend to be low and ornamental rather than high enough for strict privacy, which reduces the cost and yet still provides a firm and attractive boundary. Nor are proper bricks the only materials used: many paving manufacturers provide walling blocks that have a stone-like finish. Where a high but decorative wall is required, pierced concrete blocks can be most attractive. These can be used in conjunction with other walling materials, such as brick, to provide decorative panels.

It is often *within* the garden that walls can be used to dramatic effect: to screen a patio, act as a retaining wall, or provide raised beds.

Whether you use bricks or walling slabs (with the exception of pierced concrete blocks), the basic techniques of laying are the same.

Above left: Combination walls of brick and screen blocks allow in more light than solid brick, and yet look more substantial than screen blocks alone.

Above right: If you doubt your own ability at bricklaying, there is much to be said for starting with a low, decorative wall. It can make a good garden feature and give you confidence for more ambitious projects.

Right: A random stone wall like this one is more difficult to start with, but it shows how interesting even a low wall can be.

Left: Something for the more ambitious . . . a serpentine wall.

Buying Materials

Start by calculating exactly how many bricks or blocks you need. This is quite simple, and will avoid the cost involved in reordering a small quantity to finish the job (remember that you are likely to pay a delivery charge for these bulky items). It is worth allowing a few extra for breakages and for wastage when you have to cut them.

The standard brick is $215 \times 102 \times 65$ mm ($8\frac{1}{2} \times 4 \times 2\frac{1}{2}$ in), but remember to allow for 12 mm ($\frac{1}{2}$ in) mortar joints. Concrete-based walling is likely to come in a range of sizes, and there is no substitute for checking with the manufacturer's brochures (but do not forget to allow for the mortar).

You can buy walling blocks at many garden centres, and you will find a wide selection at a good builders' merchant, and that is where you will have to go for a choice of bricks.

There is a lot to be said for buying from the builders' merchant, as you will need sand and cement (possibly ready-mixed), and probably hardcore for foundations. It makes sense to have these delivered together.

You will have a wide choice of bricks, so choose one that is in keeping with the main buildings, and pleasing to the eye.

The walling blocks are well described in the manufacturers' leaflets, and all are obviously suitable for the job. It is different with bricks: there is a wide choice but not all are equally suitable. Always insist on one suitable for *garden* walls (which are far more vulnerable than house walls). Suitable bricks are likely to be termed 'special quality', which means that they will tolerate the wetting and freezing that paths and garden walls have to withstand. Ordinary and internal bricks are likely to ruin your workmanship after a comparatively short time.

You may also be confronted by three *varieties* of bricks: common, facing and engineering. Engineering bricks are strong and dense, but you do not really need that for garden use (and they could become slippery if you use them for a path). Common bricks are useful but plain. Facing bricks are more decorative (but remember that the finish does not say anything about the *quality* of the brick).

When bricks arrive, stack them as shown opposite, with the cement or mortar mix stored on boards to keep the sacks off the ground.

It is easier to buy dry ready-mixed mortar, which is usually available in 20 and 40 kg (44 and 88 lb) bags. For ordinary bricks allow about 40 kg (88 lb) for every 50–60 bricks. If you want to mix your own, you will need to make up a mixture of one part cement, one part lime, and six parts sharp sand.

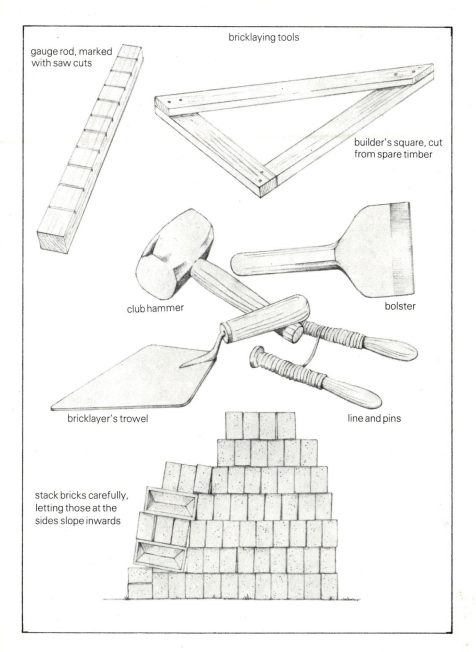

bricklaying tools

gauge rod, marked with saw cuts

builder's square, cut from spare timber

club hammer

bolster

bricklayer's trowel

line and pins

stack bricks carefully, letting those at the sides slope inwards

Foundations

All brickwork and walling blocks need a level, solid foundation. Load-bearing walls must obviously have very substantial foundations, but for most garden walls something more modest is adequate. If the wall is to be only a single brick or block wide, 13 cm (5 in) of hardcore and 15 cm (6 in) of concrete would be adequate; where the wall is to have a double thickness of brick (215 mm/$8\frac{1}{2}$ in), this ought to be increased to about 23 cm (9 in) of concrete over 13 cm (5 in) of hardcore. The finished level of this 'footing' should be about 15 cm (6 in) below soil-level in the first example, 23 cm (9 in) in the second. These foundations will be adequate for most garden walls. The width of the foundation should be about three times the width of the wall. Naturally these are only guidelines; for a low wall of perhaps only 60 cm (2 ft) the foundations can be less substantial, while for a wall 1.8 m (6 ft) or so high you would need to increase them. The stability of the subsoil might also affect your decision.

Use a mix of one part cement to five parts combined aggregate for the foundations, tamping to compact and level it. Leave it for a week to harden.

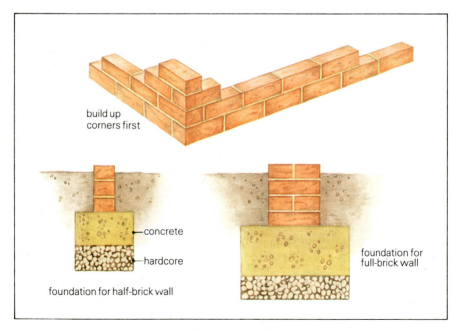

build up
corners first

concrete

hardcore

foundation for half-brick wall

foundation for
full-brick wall

How to Build a Brick Wall

Although the method described here is for bricks, the same principles apply to walling blocks, although in this case blocks of several sizes might be used.

For the courses below soil-level you should really use a strong mortar (one part cement to three parts sharp sand), though the mix previously suggested is best for above-ground joints.

Only mix enough mortar for perhaps half an hour's work, and use a 'spot-board' (a piece of wood about 60 cm or 2 ft square, which you can rest on five bricks). The consistency should be thick enough to compress to 12 mm ($\frac{1}{2}$ in) if you gently push another brick down on a 2.5 cm (1 in) layer. If it is too thick you will not be able to do this, if it is too thin it will not support the brick or block.

Put down a line so that the wall will be straight, and using a brick-layer's trowel place mortar on the concrete foundation.

Take a slice of mortar and lift it with a sweeping motion. Place the 'sausage' of mortar in the centre of the brick or block, and use the back of the trowel to roll it back and make a reasonably smooth layer about 12 mm ($\frac{1}{2}$ in) thick.

Lay an end or corner brick first. Tap it down on to the mortar bed, using the handle of the trowel, and check the level with a spirit-level. To lay the second brick or block, lay two small slices of mortar on the end of the brick, one on each vertical edge that will butt the first brick. Tap firm and check the level, also ensuring that the row is straight with the line.

Strike off surplus mortar from the joints. A boundary wall ought to be two bricks thick, otherwise it tends to look rather thin. Some of the forms can call for complicated cutting at corners, but a straight wall of English Bond (*see* p. 45) is not too complicated. Lay the two courses at once.

You may need strengthening piers every 2.4 m (8 ft) or so on single-thickness brick walls, depending on height.

Subsequent rows are laid in the same manner, but build up the corners first, several courses high, using a spirit-level to check absolute accuracy. You can then stretch a line between the two ends as a guide.

There are many ways of finishing the joints, but a raked joint is both easy to achieve and good to look at in most garden situations. After an hour or so, before the mortar is too hard, simply use a rounded piece of metal (traditionally a bucket handle) or a stick to sweep along the joint, giving a concave profile.

Lay the first row of bricks on a bed of mortar on a firm foundation.

As each brick is laid, place two sausage-shaped slices of mortar on one end.

Press the brick into place, and remove any surplus mortar from the joints as you work.

Check levels constantly — after every few bricks until you get the hang of it.

You can use the handle of the trowel to firm a brick into place or to level it.

Check both verticals and horizontals. A long spirit-level is invaluable.

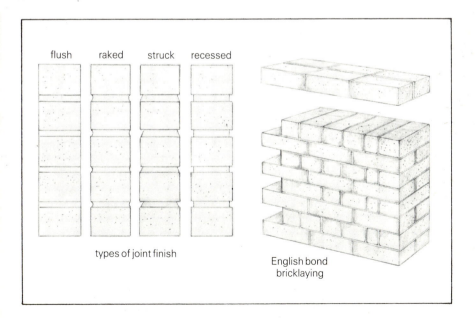

flush   raked   struck   recessed

types of joint finish

English bond bricklaying

It is often nice to finish off with suitable coping to give the whole a finished look. You can buy bricks specially for the job, and block manufacturers will also have suitable coping.

Retaining Walls

Retaining walls are sometimes inclined back slightly. The lean should be gentle: about 6 mm in 60 cm ($\frac{1}{4}$ in in 2 ft). The slope should originate from the first course, and you can check the slope by using a piece of wood 6 mm (or $\frac{1}{4}$ in) thick, together with the spirit-level. All retaining walls of any height should have 'weep' holes at the bottom; these are pipes built into the base through which water can drain.

If a retaining wall has to be built next to a brick path, it will look more harmonious if you can use the same brick.

8 Making a Patio

Patios have become very popular in recent years, probably because they have a place in almost any garden. In a large garden they can form an attractive feature that achieves a natural transition between house and garden; and on a smaller scale they can provide a garden in their own right, often being the design solution for a tiny town garden.

The patio can incorporate many additional features such as walls, raised beds and pools, and covered areas. These all add interest (an expanse of unrelieved paving is not particularly attractive), but it is the paving that makes a patio. Unless you lay this well, no amount of dressing it up will hide the problem.

Remember that it is a permanent feature, and it is better to proceed slowly (it can be quite hard work), rather than rushing the job in a weekend or two.

Concrete pavers can make an effective patio surface, and are worth considering instead of paving slabs.

Preparing the Foundations

It is tempting to skimp on the foundations, but this will only lead to trouble later.

Fortunately a patio normally only has to take light traffic. On firm ground that is not likely to shrink or move, you can simply lay on a bed of sand, but it is much better to provide a better footing.

For most uses, a 5 cm (2 in) layer of 'scalpings' (this is 2.5 cm [1 in] stone with dust, available from most builders' merchants) is adequate, or you can use compacted hardcore. If using sand alone, allow another 2.5 cm (1 in) for this, and the same depth for mortar spots. Never apply mortar directly to the earth.

The area should be excavated to the depth of the base, mortar (or sand) and thickness of slab or brick. If the paved area adjoins a house, the finished surface should be at least 15 cm (6 in) below the damp-proof course, and should slope gently to allow surface water to drain. There should be a fall of at least 5 cm in 3 m (2 in in 10 ft). Where the paving butts to the lawn, ensure that the slabs or bricks will be level with or slightly lower than the grass.

If a lot of digging and levelling is required, and you do not need the soil elsewhere, it might be worth hiring a skip. They usually take about 10.2 tonnes (10 tons), which is about 4.5-6 m³ (6-8 cu yd) of soil. If you are doing the job on your own, it will probably take you about two days to fill the skip.

If the patio is to incorporate walls, it is best to give them separate foundations instead of laying them on the edge of the actual paving. Foundations for walls are described on page 42.

If there is a lot of digging and levelling to be done, it may be worth consulting a contractor, to get most of it done mechanically.

Deciding on Materials

Paving materials are not cheap, but do not make the mistake of buying inexpensive slabs purely on cost. It may be better to make the patio small but to use more sympathetic materials that blend better with the house and garden. It is wise to calculate all your costs carefully, as individual items may not seem expensive but can soon become a major expenditure.

The main paving materials fall into three groups: pre-cast concrete slabs, interlocking concrete blocks, which are often used by local authorities but have a use in the garden too, and bricks or pavers.

There are alternatives, such as proper York stone if you can afford it or have access to a second-hand supply locally, but most of the suitable and widely available materials fall within the broad categories described.

Pre-cast concrete paving slabs sound utterly boring and uninteresting. Some of them are just this (although for some areas, such as a hard standing for a car, it may not matter), but others are both sophisticated and superb to look at.

Most patios are laid with traditional rectangular slabs with a plain finish, albeit coloured. For a little extra cost it is possible to buy them with a textured finish, such as 'rippled' (irregularly grooved, but still looking artificial) or 'riven' (a finish that attempts to reproduce the stratified surface characteristic of York stone). There are other decorative and tasteful finishes, including one type that has a finish based on Mediterranean-style stone cobbles, and the range includes a curved pattern within the square block as well as one with an arc cut out to form a tree space or bed when four are placed together. These are obviously more expensive than normal slabs, and you may not

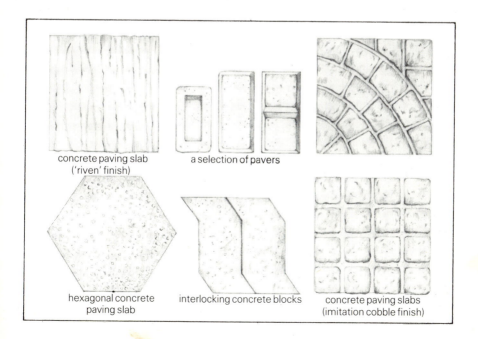

concrete paving slab
('riven' finish)

a selection of pavers

hexagonal concrete
paving slab

interlocking concrete blocks

concrete paving slabs
(imitation cobble finish)

want an uneven surface if you plan to use tables and chairs, but they demonstrate that paving need never be unimaginative.

Choice of colour can be important; you want something that will blend harmoniously with the plants and surroundings. Bright pinks can look fine for swimming pool surrounds and a formal terrace or a patio in front of a summerhouse, but rather obtrusive and harsh where plants play an important role. The house itself should also have an influence; again the bright colours might not look right against the setting of an old Elizabethan cottage, whereas a riven finish in a weathered York or even Cotswold colour would.

Colours weather and mellow anyway, of course, so try to see a sample of what the paving looks like when it has been down for six months or a year. Often the effect is quite different. Certainly the striking difference between colours in a 'patchwork' design is much more muted.

Of course the paving slabs do not have to be rectangular; hexagonals (including half-slabs for producing straight edges at the sides) can look attractive in a formal setting. There are other shapes, but these are probably best avoided for the patio. If you want relief from regular lines, choose a variety of rectangular shapes that will interlock into a pattern (some suggestions are illustrated on p. 53), or leave out the occasional large paving slab and set cobbles in concrete in them to give texture, or leave it as soil to take a shrub or other plants.

Paving slabs should be stacked so that they are not likely to be damaged and will not be a danger to people.

Always lay paving slabs on a firm base of well compacted hardcore.

Large slabs can be laid on four or five blobs of concrete (three for small ones).

Position the slabs carefully, being careful not to trap your fingers as you do so.

Use a spirit-level on each slab, tapping it level with the handle of a hammer.

Sets and pavers, including the interlocking type, have many merits. They are smaller and lighter to handle and lay, and are easier to lay to an uneven contour (not normally a problem with a small patio, but sometimes a problem with a larger paved area). They can look more 'sympathetic' in informal situations, and some closely resemble the finish of weathered bricks, one of the nicest of all finishes in a 'cottage garden' setting.

Granite sets are best avoided for a main area of paving as they have a cold appearance and tend to be hard to walk on (they are not widely available anyway). A typical paving set is about 400×200 mm (16×8 in) and 40 mm ($1\frac{1}{2}$ in) thick, making them larger but thinner than a normal brick (which is about $215 \times 102 \times 65$ mm ($8\frac{1}{2} \times 4 \times 2\frac{1}{2}$ in).

There are various finishes and shades, and some sets have the appearance of four more-or-less normal bricks, achieved with false joints.

Because colours tend to be more muted and natural anyway, many having a weathered appearance, harsh colours are not so likely to be a problem.

Paving sets have some advantages over ordinary bricks: because they are usually larger they are quicker to lay, and the finish is likely to be softer than new bricks.

Some of the interlocking concrete blocks are in a special class. They are close to brick size, but have a special shape (*see* p. 106), which enables them to be interlocked without the need for concrete. They can look mellow, and are not difficult to lay once you have acquired the technique.

Bricks can look nice if you choose the right kind. Colours range from reds, blues, yellows and browns to subtle mixtures like heather greys. They are perhaps a better choice than paving sets where you particularly want to match the brickwork of the house, or want to build matching brick walls or other features.

Because bricks used for paving will often be damp, they must be able to withstand moisture and frost; a hard, well-fired brick is likely to be best. Some bricks are smoother than others, and because these can become slippery it is probably safer to opt for a textured finish.

More suitable than ordinary bricks are clay pavers, which usually look like bricks, but are slightly different in size and can be laid on sand alone (*see* pp. 54–5). Ordinary bricks do not 'fit' properly without mortar, whereas 'flexible pavers' are designed to fit together snugly.

Some suggested patterns using paving slabs and interlocking blocks.

Opposite page, top: Imaginative use of clay pavers, but an ambitious project for a beginner.

Far left: Flexible pavers are laid on a bed of sand, tamped firm with a suitable board.

Left: Most clay flexible pavers are rectangular, but these are interlocking.

Above: Concrete interlocking blocks in a small garden.

Above right: In an isolated part of the garden, traditional paving slabs can make a bolder feature.

Right: Most garden centres offer a wide range of interesting paving materials.

Buying Paving

The best advice is to shop around before you buy, not only because prices may vary but also because the range stocked by any one outlet might be so small that you may miss the opportunity to purchase a more attractive product.

The larger garden centres will stock a reasonable range, but builders' merchants can often be a better place to go, especially if you want to consider bricks as well.

Many manufacturers offer useful leaflets, but you are likely to be referred to a local stockist to place the order. This makes sense because of the sheer weight of the product. They are normally delivered from a local stockist, and you may have to pay extra for delivery.

Because of handling and transport costs, the quantity you order can affect the price per unit; you will obviously pay more per brick if you order 500 than you would if you ordered 5,000.

It pays to work out carefully the quantity you require, allowing for one or two breakages, and order them all at once. This can be particularly important where coloured paving is involved, as there could be a slight variation in shade if some are ordered separately.

When you are buying bricks you may have a choice of solid bricks, frogged bricks or holed bricks. It is best to avoid those with holes in (or bricks with frogs on both sides), as you would have to lay them on edge (which means you need more for a given area), but single-frogged bricks can be used satisfactorily if you lay with the frog down.

When bricks or paving slabs are delivered, try to stack them on a level area such as concrete (or on scaffolding planks if you have to use an area like a lawn), and cover with a sheet of polythene to keep the rain off (some paving slabs may come shrink-wrapped, although odd slabs are bound to be loose).

Always stack paving safely, as a heavy slab can cause injury if it falls, and children are often tempted to climb. The best way to stack bricks is shown on page 41.

The Mortar

You can lay paving on sand alone. Some types are designed to lock together without mortar (*see* page 54). Mostly, though, mortar is preferred for a firm patio. Grouting between the slabs prevents weed growth.

If you prefer you can mix your own mortar, using cement and sharp

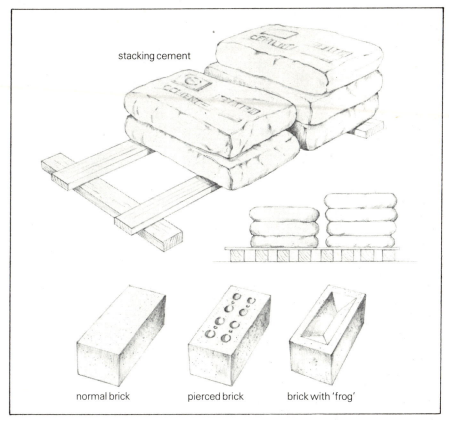

stacking cement

normal brick   pierced brick   brick with 'frog'

Store cement in a dry place and off the ground. The bricks illustrate some of the terms you might encounter.

sand, but dry ready-mixed mortar is easier to use and is probably worth the extra cost for speed and convenience, unless the area is large.

A mixture suitable for most paving jobs is 1:6 (one part cement to six parts sand). If 1:6 is not available, 1:5 is perfectly suitable. These mixes can be used both for bedding the slabs or bricks and for filling between the joints.

Only mix as much mortar as you can use within an hour. As soon as it begins to set, throw it away; do not try to add more water.

9 Pergolas and Rustic Work

You do not need to be a proficient carpenter to erect a pergola, or other rustic work, but you do need to be thorough if it is not to blow down in a gale. Without the plants on, there is not a lot of wind resistance, but once clothed with plants there is both weight and wind resistance to contend with. For that reason the upright must be secure and the joins and joints adequate.

The simplest form to tackle is a structure made from rustic poles (usually larch or fir), but it is not difficult to make a robust structure from prepared timber. For a more permanent and impressive structure, brick pillars can be used, and these can be very effective for providing a canopy over part of a patio.

Rustic poles are usually available from good garden centres, and the only tools needed are a saw, hammer, a bag of long nails, and a good idea of the design you are aiming to achieve (plus of course a spade to dig holes for the uprights, and drainpipes or concrete for firm anchorage).

For the uprights you will need poles or timbers of at least 2.4 m (8 ft): with 60 cm (2 ft) in the ground, you will still only have 1.8 m (6 ft) clearance overhead.

Sketch the structure on paper first, not only so that you will know how much to order but also to provide a clear idea of the sequence of steps when you come to build it.

It is worth treating prepared timber with a wood preservative, giving special attention to the part that goes in the ground. With rustic poles, it is worth treating the part that will be buried.

Making a Rustic Arch

An extra pair of hands is necessary to support the framework while some of the sections are being nailed together. Where possible some sections can be assembled on the ground, for instance the cross-members of the 'roof'. This makes it easier than attempting to nail all the joints *in situ*.

Start by inserting the uprights, preferably concreting them in position (*see* page 32). Once these are firmly set in position, fill in the sides. Cut the pieces to length by marking them off after holding them

When designing rustic work, always try to bear in mind what it will look like clothed with plants. Keep it simple but bold.

against the pieces they are to join. Saw the ends cleanly and drive the nail in at an angle, if necessary, to go through both sections. It may be necessary to hold a club hammer the other side to offer firm resistance as the nail is driven home.

Sloping struts, as opposed to those pieces joined at right-angles, will have to be cut at an angle. As this will vary according to the positioning of the piece, the best way is to hold it in position and mark the angle before cutting. Having got one end right, repeat for the other end.

Nailed joints are adequate for the fill-in pieces for the sides, but a roof section ought to be partially jointed as well. The horizontal pieces should have notches sawn and chiselled out (*see* p. 60) to fit over the upright before being nailed into position.

Additional bracing struts from the sides to the cross-poles will give additional strength and rigidity.

Making a Timber Pergola

Prepared timber 10 × 10 cm (4 × 4 in) should be adequate for a modest structure, though for a tall or wide design go for 15 × 15 cm (6 × 6 in). Deal, pine or cedar are all suitable.

It is best to keep the design simple: upright posts, set firmly as described for fencing post on page 32, horizontal bars linking the tops, with cross-pieces to join the two halves together and give strength.

With prepared timber, the pieces should be jointed and joined with dowels or screws. The joints should be cut and any holes drilled before the pergola is erected. Treat all timber with a preservative. A typical method of assembly is illustrated below.

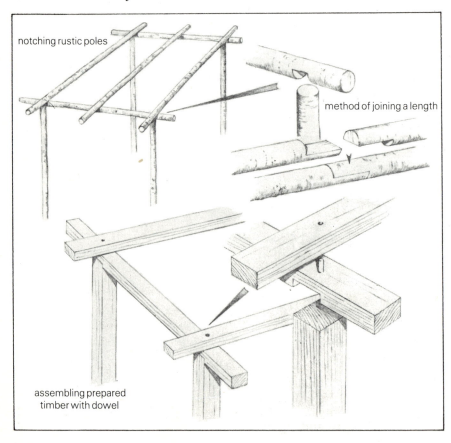

notching rustic poles

method of joining a length

assembling prepared timber with dowel

Brick and Timber

A brick and timber pergola can be particularly impressive. The problem can be one of scale; the supports must be in proportion to the cross-members. For that reason it is preferable to use more substantial timbers, such as 23 × 5 cm (9 × 2 in) softwood beams (again well treated).

The pillars must be on good foundations. To avoid too many pillars, it may be preferable to run timber of similar dimensions along between them, and to fix the cross-members to these.

There are several methods of fixing timber securely to brick pillars. Two are illustrated below; another is to set a threaded bolt long enough to go through the timber into the mortar. The timber should be pre-drilled, and the timber secured in place by tightening the nut. Use a spirit-level to check that the bolt is vertical.

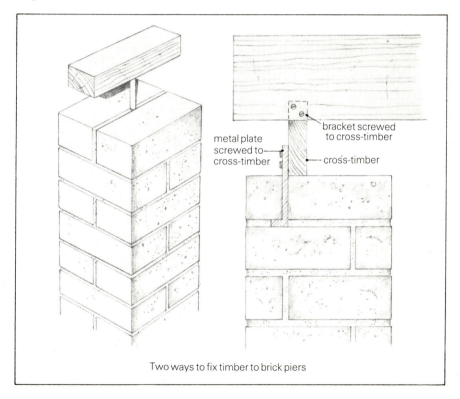

bracket screwed to cross-timber

metal plate screwed to cross-timber

cross-timber

Two ways to fix timber to brick piers

10 Making a Water Garden

The effort involved in making a concrete pool is considerable, and there is all the complication of shuttering (and steel reinforcing rods if the area is large) not to mention the special preparations before the pond is safe for stocking. As the life is not necessarily very long, the practical choice for most of us lies between flexible 'liners' and a pre-formed rigid plastic or glass-fibre pool.

Flexible liners offer the advantage of variable shape, but do not let this tempt you into intricate curves and bays: such indulgence is wasteful of material and seldom looks as effective as larger and more gentle sweeps.

As you will see from the chart on p. 69, a liner based on butyl rubber lasts a long time, and can be joined to make a pond to match the most ambitious plan (it has been used for an 18-acre reservoir!). The colour is black; if you want a stone-coloured finish you can buy one with a plastic laminate surface (but it will cost a lot more). PVC laminate with nylon reinforcement also provides a long-lasting pool, while a similar material without the nylon reinforcement gives a good life at significantly less cost. As polythene should be used at double thickness the cost saving over a PVC laminate is not really large enough to make it worth serious consideration, given its short life in comparison.

Some of the liners are blue on one side and stone-coloured on the other, giving a choice of finish. It is better to use the stone uppermost, as blue can tend to look more like a miniature swimming pool than a natural pond.

The problem with most pre-formed pools is that they are often small, despite their apparent size when standing on end in a garden centre. They tend to be shallow, and some of the outlines look fussy and mean once they are in a garden.

Making a Liner Pool

The method of construction is the same for all kinds of liner. The shape must be worked out in advance, to order the right size. You can calculate the size by taking the length of your design and adding twice the maximum depth, and adding twice the maximum depth to the width. There is no need to make special allowances for marginal'

Flexible liners are useful for small garden pools, and edged with brick they can look very solid and permanent.

shelves (to grow plants).

No pool need be more than 75 cm (2½ ft) deep. As a guide to suitable depths, 38 cm (15 in) is adequate for a surface area of about 2 m² (22 sq ft), 45 cm (1½ ft) up to 9 m² (100 sq ft), and 60 cm (2 ft) up to 18 m² (200 sq ft).

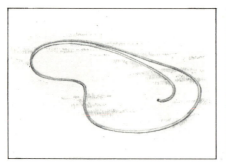

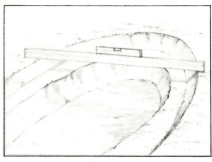

A hosepipe can be used to mark out the shape of your pool.

Always make sure the sides are level before using the liner.

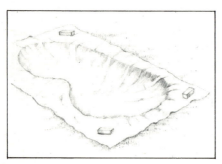

Lay the liner loosely over the pool, anchored with bricks.

Move the bricks as the water gradually fills the pool.

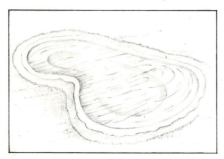

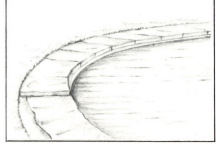

Trim off surplus liner, leaving a 15 cm (6 in) lip.

For a neat finish, top with paving or even turf.

Transfer your shape to the ground by using a hosepipe, or dribbling out the pattern in sand or lime. This is the time to make any adjustments. Once you are happy with it, you can begin to cut out the shape, keeping to the inside of the marks (you can always trim back further if necessary). If you are cutting into a lawn, it is best to remove the turf for about 30 cm (1 ft) all round, to allow for the edge to be laid in and covered. Use a spirit-level on a straight-edge to ensure that the area is level in all directions. When you are satisfied with this, excavate down about 23 cm (9 in), which will be the level of the first shelf, giving the side a slope of 20° (7.5 cm in 23 cm/3 in in 9 in). If the soil is very sandy the slope may have to be more gradual. Finally, excavate the inner area (the shelf should be about 23 cm [9 in] wide). The final depth should be no more than you calculated when you bought the liner.

Carefully check that there are no sharp stones or any large roots protruding from the excavation; if necessary line with a layer of sand, or even old newspapers. Recheck that the pool is *level*.

Drape the liner loosely over the hole, using bricks at each corner to hold it in place, then begin to run water in through a hose. As the pool fills, lift and reposition the weights occasionally. For rectangular pools it is necessary to tuck pleats in the corners to make it neat.

When the pond is full, trim off surplus liner, leaving a 10 cm (4 in) overlap.

How you finish the edge is a matter of taste. Paving slabs are popular, but tend to give an unnatural appearance. Crazy-paving is better, but you can even have lawn or soil up to the edge. A bed of soil in which to make a pond-side planting can be particularly attractive. Because loose soil will just slip into the pond, finish off by placing inverted turves over the overlapped edge, then spread fine soil over these.

Installing a Rigid Pool

Excavating the holes for these can sometimes be tricky if the shape is a complicated one. For semi-rigid vacuum-formed weather-resistant plastic pools, lay the pool, right way up, where it is to go, and use a stick or something sharp to scribe the outline (taking the outer edge of the rim) on the ground. For glass-fibre pools, add an extra 15 cm (6 in) on all sides. The hole should be 2.5 cm (1 in) deeper than the pool (and if you are finishing with paving round the edge, allow for this). You will not be able to excavate the hole to the exact shape if the pool has marginal shelves as well as complicated curves, so take out the whole area to the full depth.

Place 2.5 cm (1 in) of sand at the bottom, then position the pool, using a spirit-level and straight-edge to check that it is level in all directions. Gradually start to back-fill the cavity with sand or sifted soil, compacting it well, especially beneath the shelves. With semi-rigid plastic pools, fill the pool with water at the same rate as you compact the soil or sand round the outside. With glass-fibre pools, fill once the packing has been completed. Check for level as you proceed.

It is important to install a rigid pool carefully, making sure it is firmly supported ... and level. Mark out the shape as carefully as you can, excavate a little more than the size of the pool; line with sand, and be prepared to backfill afterwards.

Cascades and Fountains

A still pool adds charm to any garden, but moving water provides an extra dimension. The combination of movement and sound add much to the pleasures of water gardening. The cost could well double the initial price of your pool, but installation is quite simple.

In an ideal site the pool would be at the bottom of a natural slope, for

pump chamber

If you have a large pool with cascades and fountain, you may need a pump in a separate chamber outside the pool. For small pools, however, a submersible pump will probably be adequate.

a cascade or waterfall, but it is often a case of creating height by making a rock garden down which the water can cascade. If you are using a semi-rigid or glass-fibre preformed pool it is probably best to use cascade dishes of the same material.

If a flexible liner has been used for the pool, the more natural appearance that can be created with a liner cascade is likely to look better. Even if a PVC liner has been used for the pool, you will find that butyl is easier to mould into shape for the waterfalls. You can use several small pieces as shown in the diagram, provided that the join is above the water level. Each mini-pool must have a backward slope to hold water even when the pump is not running; about 10 cm (4 in) of

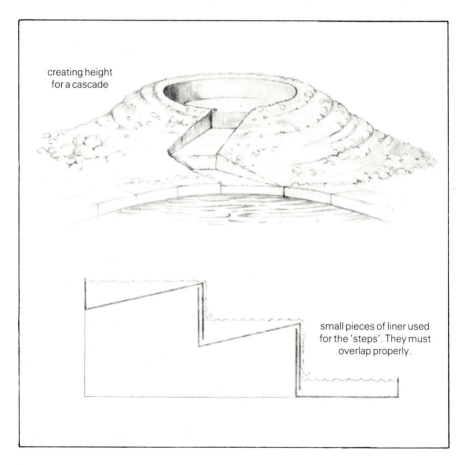

creating height for a cascade

small pieces of liner used for the 'steps'. They must overlap properly.

water is about the minimum to aim for. The positioning of rocks or stones will dictate the shape and flow of the fall. Fix them in place with mortar.

The choice of pump can be a difficult one, and it is best to seek expert advice from a water garden specialist, explaining exactly what you want it to do. The notes here are only guidelines, and the capacity and merits of each pump must be taken individually.

There is a choice of submersible or surface pump. Submersible pumps are the easiest for small pools; there is no need for a separate pump chamber to be constructed, and no plumbing between pool and pump. A surface pump will be required where a relatively high head is required, or several fountains. Most pumps operate at mains voltage, but low-voltage models running at 24 volts are available, complete with transformer (which is located safely away from the pool).

If in doubt about wiring, consult an electrician. Further advice, and information on installing underwater lighting, will be found on pp. 86-8.

Likely Life Expectancy for Various Materials

Material	Estimated life	Cost index*
Heavy-gauge polythene (double thickness)	1-2 years	1
Laminated PVC	5-10 years	1.1
Laminated PVC with nylon reinforcement	10 years	1.9
Butyl (0.03 in gauge)	50 years	2.2
Concrete	2-20 years	2.3
Butyl with stone-coloured plastic laminate	50 years	3.6

*These are approximate costs at time of writing, based on the prices charged by a leading water garden specialist, for a pool about 2.4 m × 1.5 m × 45 cm (8 ft × 5 ft × 1½ ft). You may be able to buy polythene cheaper from a polythene supplier. The thickness of many of the materials will also affect comparative prices.
1 is the cost of double thickness heavy-gauge polythene (laminated PVC with nylon reinforcement would cost just under twice the amount, for example).
Note: PVC and butyl liners can be repaired with inexpensive repair kits.

11 Sheds and Summerhouses

Although most sheds are purely traditional in outline, some are quite well designed and the borderline between shed and summerhouse can become a thin one. They are all major garden purchases, and you should spend time looking round display grounds before deciding on the model.

There are two principal forms of garden shed: those with an apex roof (an inverted V) and those with a pent roof (usually sloping from front to back in one piece). The apex roof tends to look right in an open part of the garden, whereas the pent style is often more suitable if it is positioned against or near a wall.

You will usually have more headroom in an apex type, but not invariably. If you are likely to spend much time in it, do try them out inside; insufficient clearance can be distressing, and cross-braces can be in just the right position to crack your head against.

Most doors are about 75 cm ($2\frac{1}{2}$ ft) wide. If you have wide garden machinery, check that there is adequate clearance.

Timber is the most popular choice of material for both sheds and summerhouses, because it blends into a garden setting. Properly treated with a preservative it is long-lasting, but quality is very variable and you will probably get what you pay for. The cheapest kinds are usually made from deal (some manufacturers use the terms softwood or whitewood: European redwood can also come under this loose heading). All these should be treated with a wood preservative. Some companies charge extra for this, and it can add $7\frac{1}{2}$–10 per cent to the price. Western red cedar, which is a more expensive wood, can be left untreated, although colour will be improved by using a cedar preparation.

There are several forms of cladding, and some of them are illustrated on p. 72.

Timber is not the only possibility for a garden shed; metal or concrete are other options. Concrete may sound appalling in a garden setting, but many of us tolerate concrete garages, and if sited in close proximity to similar buildings it is a possibility. Metal sheds are not very popular either, but they can be quite pleasing in the right situation. They tend to have a low-pitched apex roof. Many have the advantage of reasonable price.

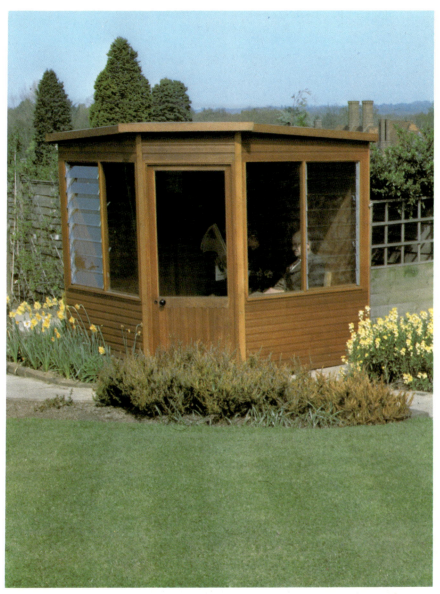

Somewhere out of the wind to sit and enjoy the garden on a cold spring day. .

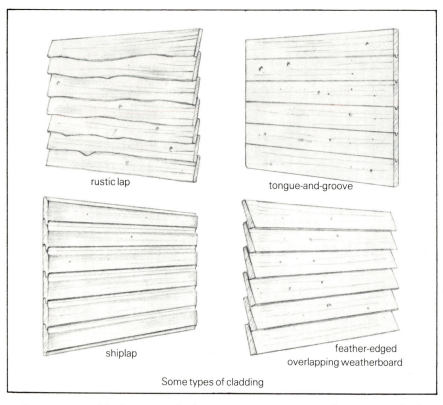

rustic lap

tongue-and-groove

shiplap

feather-edged
overlapping weatherboard

Some types of cladding

You are not likely to need planning permission unless your shed or summerhouse is going to take up half of your garden, or you want to site it in the front garden (and there are certain other unlikely situations that could cause problems). A telephone call to the planning department of your local authority will resolve any doubts. Building regulations also have to be considered, and you should not have the structure within 2 m of the house.

Erection

Many companies will erect sheds or summerhouses for you, but they are not difficult to handle yourself if you have that invaluable extra pair of hands. It is simply a matter of bolting the sections together according to the instructions supplied. They should come complete

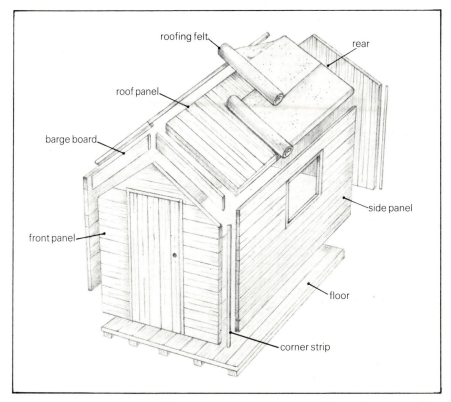

with roofing felt, glass, and any other items you will need to complete the job.

For concrete sheds you will need a concrete base, and you should follow the manufacturer's advice on the exact size of this and how to lay it. Most wooden sheds and summerhouses are simply laid on firm, level ground. You should, however, use specially treated 'bearers' (usually an extra cost) to prevent dampness being a problem. These are stout pieces of timber, usually about 7.5 × 5 cm (3 × 2 in), that have been pressure impregnated with a preservative.

For a 1.8 m (6 ft) wide building, three rows of bearers are normally required, four rows for a 2.4 m (8 ft) wide structure. Floors are sometimes an extra, but are an essential unless you use a concrete base (in which case the manufacturer will advise).

A good manufacturer will provide rustproof bolts and nails. If these are not provided it is worth buying them yourself.

12 Greenhouses

A greenhouse is a major garden purchase. Yet chosen wisely it can enhance the garden and extend the range of gardening activities.

Most greenhouses bought are of the free-standing style, although lean-to structures are well worth considering if you have a sunny (preferably south-facing) wall you can use. Some of the more ornate and elaborate designs are practically conservatories. Even the free-standing styles can be obtained in graceful, modern outline. You pay more for the design of course, and if you just want to grow a few tomatoes in the summer, perhaps followed by chrysanthemums, and maybe raise bedding plants in spring, then a traditional style may be perfectly adequate.

Do not overlook the possibility of unusual shapes such as octagons and domes for patios or if you want to make a garden feature of it.

They have drawbacks for general use, but the problems might be outweighed in these situations.

Aluminium alloy greenhouses are by far the most popular; they are virtually maintenance-free, long-lasting, and because the glazing bars are narrow they let through more light. Aluminium alloy greenhouses are likely to be glazed to the ground.

Timber-framed greenhouses need regular maintenance, but are still preferred by some gardeners because of their rustic appearance. Whether you choose a structure with glass to the ground, or one with a timber or brick base, should depend on the crops you intend to grow. If it is mainly for pot plants, there is a lot to be said for a solid base, but crops like tomatoes will benefit from the extra light resulting from full glazing.

Cedar is a popular choice of timber, and it has the benefit of natural rot resistance, and does not warp easily. Softwoods such as deal are much less expensive, but you will have to paint the wood regularly.

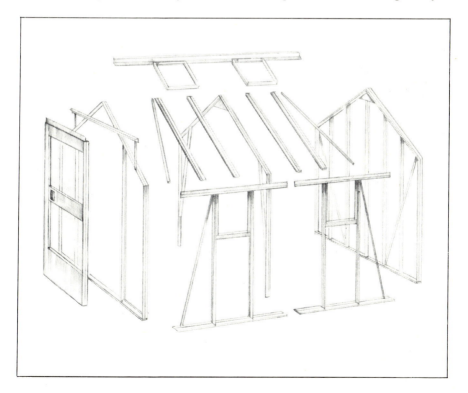

Metal bases usually have anchors to be concreted in.

Easy-to-use spring clips make glazing very simple.

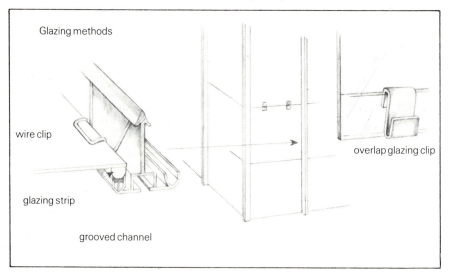

Glazing methods

wire clip

glazing strip

grooved channel

overlap glazing clip

Erecting a Greenhouse

Although greenhouses are not too difficult to erect, an extra pair of hands for the critical stages is almost essential. It is likely to take one or two days to erect once you have the foundations ready.

Most aluminium greenhouses sit on a special base, which you anchor into the ground. You will find that most manufacturers offer the base as an extra, and you have the choice of buying this or providing proper foundations. It is easier to buy the base. Some of the more expensive models actually include a built-in base.

The one essential for all greenhouses is firm, *level* ground. If the ground is in the least unstable, excavate a trench 30 cm (1 ft) deep, fill it with hardcore and sand, then top with concrete or paving slabs. But before you do this check with the manufacturer first. In a windy, exposed site it is well worth using a foundation and setting the anchors in concrete, but elsewhere it may be perfectly adequate to drive the fixing anchors into firm ground.

If you are going to build a brick base, then proper foundations are essential. Check with the manufacturer the exact dimensions, and lay both foundations and bricks as described for walls (*see* pages 38-46).

The Legal Aspects

A lean-to greenhouse erected against the house may be subject to building regulations permission. It is extremely unlikely that you will have problems with the construction materials but the regulations also cover things like proximity to the boundary.

If it will bring the total area of extensions (including garages) over a certain figure, you will need to have planning permission.

A telephone call to your local authority will clarify the position.

Some manufacturers will erect the greenhouse for you, and this is included in the price, but they will probably expect the site and any foundations to be ready for them.

If you erect it yourself the framework will probably arrive packed flat, in a number of boxes. The glass may arrive separately (possibly a few days later). Some models come ready glazed, but although it saves time on a tricky part of the job, the sections can be heavy and difficult to handle.

Assembly is really a case of following the manufacturer's instructions, and nothing more elaborate than a screwdriver and a spanner is normally required. A good, long spirit-level will help you check the vertical and horizontal levels (which should be done frequently).

Glazing is usually done with glazing clips on metal-framed greenhouses and this speeds the job, but do not rush it. Putty or glazing clips, together with instructions for use, will be supplied. You might be given a spare pane of glass too, just in case!

13 Children's Corner

A wise parent will provide a small portion of the garden in which children can be encouraged to grow things. This ought to be in a sunny, open area, not tucked away beneath a tree in a corner where nothing will grow — the surest way to snuff out the flame of enthusiasm. The play area, however, can be in an inconspicuous part of the garden; the children will probably prefer the privacy and it will not spoil the effect of the garden.

Swings, slides and climbing frames must be safe, and as they are difficult to make anyway are best bought. Any fixing instructions come with the product. What they probably will not tell you is what to do about the lawn beneath say a swing or see-saw, which will soon be

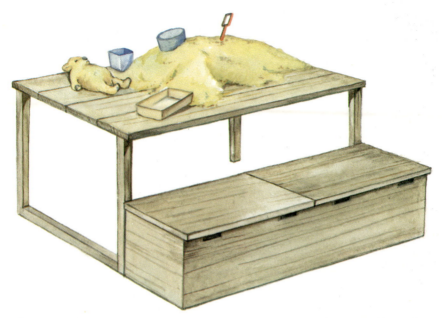

Anyone handy with wood should be able to make a simple play table with storage space for toys.

transformed to a muddy rut in wet weather or a dust-bowl in dry weather. The answer is to lay down a piece of thick green plastic netting (not the flimsy type), fixing it firmly to the base of the frame, and possibly pegging it down with thick bent wire pegs if necessary. This will offer some protection, and you can still mow over it.

If you are a handyman by nature you may want to try making your own Wendy house, although there are some attractive buildings for children that you can buy if you prefer this.

Two quite simple play items you can make yourself are a small sand pit and a useful play table. The play table can be made from scrap wood that you may have available, as dimensions can be whatever suits your materials. It is simply a table top (but make sure that it is reasonably weatherproof; chipboard, for instance, seems strong, but will not stand up to the constant dampness), supported at each end with legs strengthened by cross-members at the bottom. The seat should be fixed to the table to provide additional strength to the unit. If you hinge the box-type seat, you will have a useful place to store outdoor toys.

14 Garden Seats

A garden that lacks somewhere to sit suggests one where it is all work and no relaxation. Even though working in the garden is an active hobby, there seems little point if you cannot eventually sit down and relax in it to appreciate your efforts.

You can buy garden furniture, of course. Some of it is basic (though not cheap), such as a wooden seat; some elegant and sophisticated, in materials that range from cast-metal to plastic. Too much of it can make the garden look like a furniture showroom. Seats that are built into the garden design, however, can blend in as part of the garden setting.

Bench seats are particularly easy to incorporate into a patio. Perhaps the simplest way is to cap a low wall with paving slabs. They form a completely weatherproof seat and it is a simple matter to bring out a cushion when you want to use the seat. You have a wide choice of

Stone seats look uncomfortable, but often they are only used for a short time . . . and you can always use a cushion!

Stone and timber can make a particularly pleasing combination. You can tailor-make the seat to suit the space.

bricks and walling blocks for walls, which should be laid the right distance apart for the size of slab, and on properly prepared foundations (*see* page 42). It is sometimes more effective if the slab overlaps the front of the wall slightly.

Height should be about 30-45 cm (1-1½ ft), and there is no necessity for a 'back' on a bench seat. However, if there are raised beds incorporated into the design, it often looks better if these can be used to frame the seat (*see* above).

Sometimes a timber finish to the seat is more desirable, especially where there is perhaps matching timber in other parts of the patio. Always buy well seasoned timber; ideally at least 2.5 cm (1 in) thick, and each plank a minimum of 15 cm (6 in) wide. Try to avoid joining lengths, but if the seat is simply too long stagger the joints. Always treat the timber well with a preservative (especially important if an inexpensive softwood is being used). Fix the timber to the brickwork by drilling with a masonry drill and using a wall plug to screw into. A finishing coat of white paint usually improves the appearance.

81

15 Making a Barbecue

You can save yourself some time and buy a barbecue. You can make one for much less, and you will probably get a lot more satisfaction out of it. If you have not got a permanent site for it of course you may prefer the portable commercial type but if you have the space and enjoy eating in the open air then it is not difficult to make one that is part of the garden scene.

You will almost certainly choose brick, which is easy to build with and has the right kind of appearance. You can build a more permanent type, or quickly improvise one in the way described below.

Step One Ideally you should use special quality bricks suitable for outdoor use (tell the merchant what you want them for). Lay the first course of six bricks as shown here, making sure the ground is firm and level.

Step Two Stagger the bricks in each layer until you have reached the required height (about ten courses), then place a sheet of metal, cut to shape, over the top (your garage may help with the sheet of metal).

Step Three The last course requires a 23 cm (9 in) gap, so you will have to cut a brick in half (*see* below) and use the two halves as shown here. You can place a brick on edge in the gap to control the draught.

Step Four Place a grill from the household cooker over the last row of bricks and use four bricks to form a framework round three sides of it. The barbecue illustrated required 64 bricks.

For the temporary barbecue shown on the opposite page, you will need to cut a brick. This is easy to do with a bolster and heavy hammer if you use a bed of sand. Tap round the brick to score it first, then strike the bolster firmly along the scored line.

16 Electricity in the Garden

Electricity is a wonderful servant. It can also be deadly if not treated with respect. In the garden it is especially exposed to dampness and the risk of accident; for these reasons special care must be taken when using electricity in the garden. If you are in the slightest doubt call in a qualified electrician. If you are worried about the cost, it is sometimes possible to arrange that you will do some of the labour-intensive but non-skilled work, such as taking out a trench for laying a cable. Within the space given to the subject in this book, it is impossible to cover it in depth, but it should give you an idea of the nature of the work involved. If you want to do the work yourself, check specifications, explaining exactly what you want the materials for, with your electrical supplier. If you are reasonably competent and seek advice for the specific work you have in hand, it is not a difficult job, but even so it is a good idea to get a qualified electrician to inspect the system before it is connected to the mains — a job you will probably have to get the electricity board to do anyway.

Any separate building (greenhouse, shed, garage) must have its own power supply independent of circuits in the house, and it must be taken as an extension service from the normal domestic supply. Garden lighting, and pumps for fountains and waterfalls, must also have a separate permanent supply from individual circuits (some low-voltage systems can be run from a transformer indoors and supplied from the normal circuit).

Under certain circumstances, the special cable can be taken over-head, supported on a catenary, but as this is quite a specialized thing to erect, and hardly looks attractive, it is probably better to concentrate on the other alternative, a buried cable.

Three types of cable can be used underground: special PVC-insulated conductors plus an earth conductor, mineral-insulated copper-clad cable, and armoured PVC-insulated and sheathed cable. The first of these must be run in conduit (galvanized steel or special rigid PVC), and for ease of installation the choice usually lies with one of the alternatives.

Mineral-insulated copper-clad cable (MICC for short), is thinner in cross-section, which can be useful when it comes to feeding cables through holes, or if you do not want anything too obtrusive where it is

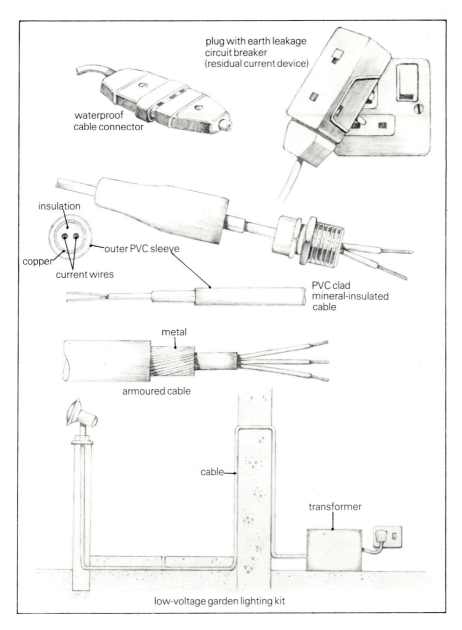

plug with earth leakage
circuit breaker
(residual current device)

waterproof
cable connector

insulation

copper

current wires

outer PVC sleeve

PVC clad
mineral-insulated
cable

metal

armoured cable

cable

transformer

low-voltage garden lighting kit

visible. Armoured cable must have a special gland fixed to the end, and can be fitted with a wrench and pliers. MICC cables need a special seal fitted to the end, and you may also need to have a screwed gland fixed. Because special tools are required for fitting MICC seals, it is best to have these fitted when you order the cable. If you do, it is important to measure accurately beforehand. You may find that you have to go to an *electric wholesaler* for suitable outdoor cable and waterproof fittings.

At the house end, it is usually convenient to terminate in a junction box inside where the special cable can be joined to easier-to-install domestic indoor cable of the correct rating. This can be used for the rest of the run to a separate switch fuse, or if a switch only then it might be possible to run a cable to a spare fuseway on the main consumer unit (the main fusebox). Otherwise it may be necessary to get the electricity board to wire it in. It is always advisable to consult them anyway. At the garden end, the cable must always terminate in weatherproof fittings.

If you are running a cable underground, you will need to excavate a trench at least 50 cm (20 in) deep, carefully removing any sharp stones that might damage the cable. If the cable is to run through an area likely to be cultivated, the trench should be deeper. In a vegetable plot in particular the cable should be both deep and protected with a protective tile covering. Generally it is best to run the trench along the edge of a path or flower bed (cutting through a lawn is likely to leave a permanent scar).

Even though the immediate uses may only demand a cable of 20A rating (2.5 mm²), it is worth using 30A rating (4 mm²), as the cost is not much more and it saves all the job of cable-laying if you want to use more equipment later that would increase the load.

In a greenhouse it is best to run the supply into a control panel (you can buy these from specialist greenhouse equipment suppliers) protected by a residual current device (RCD). Position the control panel where it is not likely to be splashed with water, and all the sockets run from it must be fused. Always use weatherproof plugs, and never use adaptors in a greenhouse. The new British wiring regulations now require residual current devices (RCDs, also known as current-operated earth-leakage circuit breakers) to be fitted to all circuits supplying outdoor sockets.

For mains pumps used in ponds the supply is normally taken to a chamber near the pool, where a waterproof connection is made either to a lead supplied with the pump or lighting equipment or to a transformer for a low-voltage system.

86

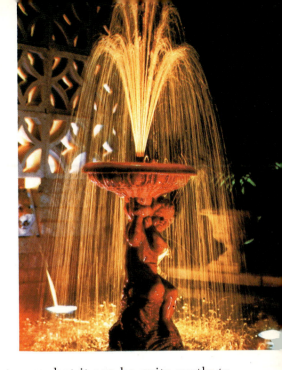

Garden lighting and moving water make an ideal combination, and once you have laid on a safe power supply you have plenty of scope. Low-voltage pond lighting kits are readily available.

Lighting

Garden lighting is not expensive to run, but it can be quite costly to install if you run a mains system and do not already have an outdoor supply for the greenhouse or for power tools. There are relatively inexpensive low-voltage systems, however, that can overcome some of the problems.

Functional lamps on gateposts and for driveways are best run on a main supply fed by an armoured cable run under the ground. Porch lights, however, can usually be run from the domestic supply by taking ordinary cable through a wall and using a weatherproof fitting. It may also be possible to run a mains cable through the wall to a *weatherproof* 13 amp socket on the outside wall for patio lights.

Some lighting systems suitable for illuminating garden features are run at 110 volts through a transformer (which you should buy from the lighting manufacturer). Keep the transformer under cover and the 240 volt connection short.

Best of all if you want garden lights without a lot of expense or trouble are the 12 volt systems. You will not have as much choice of fittings, and the output from the transformer may limit the number of lights you use, but they are easy to install.

You can keep the transformer indoors (perhaps in the garage) and run the 12 volt cable into the garden. This does not even have to be

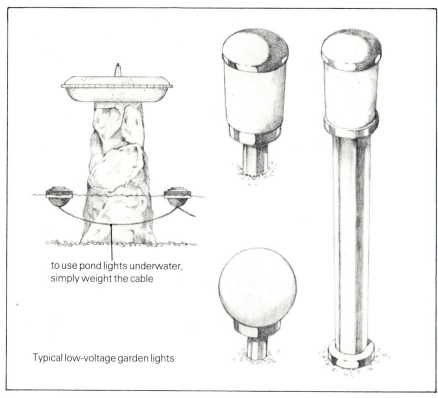

to use pond lights underwater,
simply weight the cable

Typical low-voltage garden lights

buried, and you have a flexible system that you can move about the garden. With some types, lamps can even be screwed into the system at any point you choose, and there are usually wall brackets and ground spikes in the kit.

Pond lights can be run from the same 12 volt system, but *you must buy special underwater lamps*. These are sealed, waterproof units that normally float but can be weighted to give submerged lighting too.

A Socket for Power Tools

It may be desirable to have sockets of the weatherproof type for operating power tools. These can be fixed to a post or wall, being fed in the manner already described. Such circuits should have a 30 ma residual-current device (earth-leakage circuit-breaker) for positive safety (though if used in the greenhouse these safety devices can keep 'tripping' and spoil the crops).

17 Providing a Water Supply

It is quite simple to fit an outside tap using modern compression fittings. A hacksaw and spanner are the only tools required for the actual plumbing part, with a hammer and cold chisel or 15 mm ($\frac{5}{8}$ in) 'stardrill' to make the hole through the wall to take the supply outside.

You can buy a kit containing all the necessary fittings, or you can purchase individual items from a plumber's merchant.

Turn the water off at the rising main, saw through the rising main to take the compression T-junction and tighten the compression joints. Run a short length of pipe, then insert the new stop-cock, and simply take the pipe through a hole made in the wall.

To take the supply further into the garden, it is simply a case of a longer length of pipe, and using compression elbows where you need to turn a corner.

Fitting an outside tap could affect your water rates, so you should check with your local water authority.

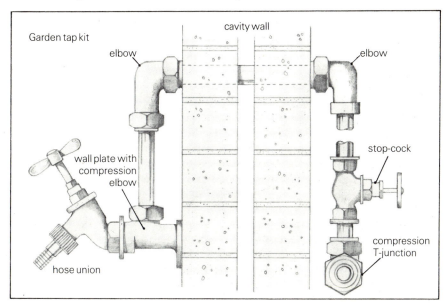

Garden tap kit — cavity wall — elbow — elbow — wall plate with compression elbow — stop-cock — hose union — compression T-junction

18 Making a Rock Garden

In the days when gardens were created on the grand scale, no self-respecting gardener would make do with anything less than several lorry loads of mountain rocks when constructing a rock garden. Such monumental earthworks are fine in a botanic garden or public park, but are hardly in keeping with the average garden today.

Also to be avoided are the unimaginative and unplanned heaps of rubble that sometimes masquerade as rockeries.

In an ideal world we would all have a garden with a natural south-facing slope, as this is likely to provide the two key requirements: full sun and good drainage. As few of us can provide the ideal, compromise is usually inevitable. Never, however, settle for a shady site — least of all beneath trees.

Resist the temptation to build an 'island mound' rock garden unless you have the space to make it work, and can afford the considerable amount of stonework that such a large bed requires. It is better to make a flat or slightly sloping bed of scree and rocks (*see* page 96) if the island bed is small, or to utilize some other garden feature as a backing and have a single-faced rock garden.

Most rock plants will be happy in a mixture of three parts garden soil, two of peat or leafmould, and one-and-a-half of sand or grit. If peat is used, choose a fine grade of moss peat in preference to sedge peat; leafmould is obviously cheaper if a supply of leaves is available, but they must be well decomposed. Particular care must be taken with the sand. Soft sand used by builders for concrete and mortar is totally unsuitable; it must be sharp (rather coarse and angular). If suitable sand is not readily available, fine, sharp grit can be substituted.

Add 3 kg of bonemeal for each cubic metre of compost (5 lb to every cubic yard), and mix all the ingredients thoroughly.

If this seems to be a lot of work, remember that a rock garden will last for many years, and that the success of most rock plants depends very much on a good soil.

The basic compost will suit most rock plants, and the only major group that will need special treatment are the lime-haters.

Rock gardens are ideally built on sloping ground, but you can have a colourful rock garden on a flat site.

It is natural to underestimate the amount of soil required, and as it is always frustrating to run out of a supply half-way through the construction be sure to mix enough. As a guide, one tonne (ton) of rock will probably need about one cubic metre (yard) of soil, although less might be needed on a sloping site.

The Rocks

The rocks themselves are the most important element in the visual appearance of any rock garden, and often the most expensive part.

You will usually have to go to a stone merchant (they normally sell pre-cast paving slabs and other garden materials), a special garden materials supplier, or a good builders' merchant.

Economically, it makes sense to confine your choice to stone stocked by a local merchant. He may stock several kinds, including stone quarried locally; this usually has the merit of being a little cheaper, and is likely to blend with the natural surroundings of the district.

There will be wide regional variations, but you may have a choice of a sandstone, a limestone and perhaps a local stone.

Limestone is best for lime-loving plants such as aubrieta, dianthus, and gypsophila, but if mainly lime-hating plants are to be grown a sandstone should be chosen.

Tufa is an unusual stone, being very porous yet moisture-absorbent, and is much lighter than ordinary stone, bulk for bulk. Because of its absorbent nature it is best to buy this stone during a dry spell if it is being sold by weight! Although lime is present, it is in a form that lime-hating plants appear not to find objectionable. Unfortunately tufa is a very pale, almost glaring, colour for the first year or two, although it improves with weathering.

As a broad guide, one cubic metre (yard) of sandstone is sufficient for about 4 m² (5 sq yd) of rockery. This is about the smallest quantity needed for a small rock garden, but if just a few rocks are required to add interest to a scree or for a small island bed they can be bought in 50 kg (hundredweight) amounts.

Construction

Drainage is of prime importance, but the ground must also be clear of perennial weeds; once the rocks are in place it can be very difficult to remove the roots of perennial weeds. Annual weeds, and newly-emerged perennials, can be controlled easily before planting by applying a weedkiller such as glyphosate, but do not use a weedkiller that will remain active in the soil.

Excavate the ground to at least 30 cm (1 ft) and incorporate rubble and hardcore that may assist drainage, ideally sloping the trench to a natural outlet for the water. On a raised site it is not necessary to excavate to this depth, as most of the drainage core can be built up within the mound. It is wise to use plenty of small rubble as well as larger pieces, otherwise the spaces between the large pieces will just be filled with soil.

For an authentic rock garden, height is important, but often that is not possible on a small site.

The prepared soil should be heaped to the approximate outline of the desired rockery, and the largest stones positioned first. As each site and every stone is different, there can be no stone-by-stone explanation of how to assemble the rocks. Nevertheless there are a few basic principles.

Never simply lay rocks on the surface; there should be plenty beneath the surface as well as above. Arrange each rock so that the grain lies horizontally, and ensure that they follow a basic line, to produce a tiered effect.

Each rock should slope back slightly, so that the rainwater runs behind the rock, and also to create better planting pockets. Try to ensure that there are vertical crevices as well as flat planting pockets.

As each rock is positioned (large ones should be manoeuvred into place with a crowbar) ram the soil firmly around it to eliminate air pockets.

Left: Granite. Not widely used for rock gardens, but right for some alpines.

Below left: Carboniferous limestone. Quite a popular choice, but not all plants will like the alkalinity.

Opposite page: Making a small rock garden (using a sandstone). Try to place the rocks in approximately the right position before you start, leaving plenty of planting space, and bearing in mind that much of the rock will be buried. Firm the soil around and beneath the rocks before you attempt to plant anything. To ensure good drainage, place sand or grit in the planting holes, and position the plants so that some of them will scramble over the rocks.

19 Making a Scree

A scree bed can form part of a large rock garden or be a feature in its own right. Because it must be well drained, excavate the site to a depth of 60 cm (2 ft), and place at least 15 cm (6 in) of rubble at the bottom, then cover this with gravel. The soil mixture recommended for rock gardens (*see* page 90) can then be used to bring it up to the level required.

For the finishing touch, dress the surface with gravel or small stone chippings, but be sure to use the right kind of material for the plants to be grown: limestone chippings are ideal for lime-loving plants, granite chippings or gravel will suit the rest.

To make the scree more interesting, a few small rocks can be set into the gravel, again sloping at a consistent angle, as with the rock garden. This is an ideal way to use any rocks you may have around the garden that would otherwise be unsuitable or insufficient for a proper rock garden.

20 Making a Peat Garden

If your interest lies in acid-loving plants yet your soil is unsuitable for them, the solution is to create local conditions that will suit them. For one or two large specimens this can be done by incorporating plenty of peat into the planting hole and regularly dressing with a peat mulch. For some of the choicer small acid-loving plants of alpine stature, the answer is to make a peat bed, where the special conditions can be created.

The bed should be arranged in tiers, rather like a rock garden, using peat blocks in place of rocks. It is sometimes possible to incorporate a peat section as part of a large rock garden, and many of the plants are perfectly in keeping with alpine plants.

The problem is finding a supplier of peat blocks. You are unlikely to find them at a garden centre, but it is worth looking at the classified advertisements in gardening magazines.

An alternative (only helpful if you have a local supply) is inverted heather turves.

For the general soil mixture, use two parts moss peat to one part lime-free soil and one part sand or grit.

If you want to grow acid-loving plants and your soil is unsuitable, you can build up a peaty bed using peat blocks.

21 Paths and Drives

Paths and drives are the backbone of the garden. They dictate the shape, to a large extent, and the materials of which they are made, and the style of laying, set the tone of the garden, whether it be modern or cottage-garden, formal or informal.

There are many variations on a theme; a brick path can be laid in perhaps half a dozen basic patterns, and the actual size, colour and texture of the bricks or paver will also influence the final appearance.

The actual choice of material and pattern must be a matter of design; the fundamentals of laying paths and drives remain the same.

The principal difference to remember when laying a drive is that it is not only wider than a path but it also has to take a much greater load (not only your car but possibly heavy commercial vehicles, even fuel tankers if you have oil-fired heating). For that reason concrete is popular, although for better appearance paving slabs bedded in concrete are often used.

Cold asphalt has its uses for drives, but is too unsympathetic for garden paths. Gravel, on the other hand, is equally at home on a drive or informal path. Bricks and clay pavers (thin bricks intended for paving) are normally thought of as more suitable for patios or cottage-garden paths, yet the 'flexible' paving systems now being more extensively developed (these are simply laid on sand, *see also* pages 54–55) will take a double-decker bus without damage, and certainly anything you are likely to have coming up your drive.

Other types of surface, such as grass, can only be used for paths, of course.

Laying concrete

Concrete sounds totally unappealing, and hard work to lay. In fact it can make a perfectly acceptable finish in the right situation, once it has weathered, and provided that it has been laid properly so that it does not have unsightly cracks. A concrete mixer is worth hiring if you have a large area to lay. If it is very large then it may be worth obtaining prices for ready-mixed concrete. Obtain quotations to see whether the cost is sufficient to justify the time and effort saved.

For non load-bearing paths, an 8 cm (3 in) depth of concrete over a hardcore base will be sufficient, but for loads of up to 0.5 tonnes

Bricks are useful for curved paths, and are easy to lay.

($\frac{1}{2}$ ton) this should be increased to 10 cm (4 in), and to 15 cm (6 in) for loads over this weight.

You can also use a special dye that you mix in if you do not like the colour of plain concrete — but use dyes with discretion. Certainly do a small test piece first, as it will probably dry a slightly different shade from the wet mix.

Laying concrete

Step One   Excavate to sufficient depth, then lay and consolidate the hardcore, having positioned shuttering (suitable old timber) and levelled it to the correct height. If the ground is level, ensure a slight fall to one side by having the shuttering on one side a little lower than the other. Use a small block under the straight-edge to ensure levels.

Step Two   Divide the path into manageable sections if it is long. Use more shuttering to provide temporary stop boards. Shovel in the concrete mix (one part cement to six parts combined aggregate). Mound it about 5 cm (2 in) higher than the shuttering, and use a tamping board to firm the concrete. Lay about 1 m (1 yd) at a time, and use a sawing motion with the board to level.

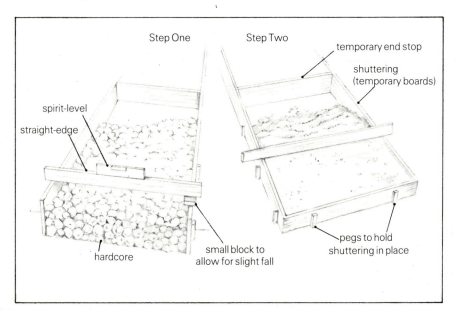

Step One   Step Two

temporary end stop

shuttering
(temporary boards)

spirit-level

straight-edge

hardcore

small block to
allow for slight fall

pegs to hold
shuttering in place

Laying gravel

Step One   Gravel is easy to lay. Start by excavating the ground to take 8 cm (3 in) of compacted hardcore and about 8 cm (3 in) of gravel; 5 cm (2 in) is adequate for many paths receiving light use. If necessary, position shuttering or kerbstones at this stage.

Step Two   Spread about half the gravel over the area, taking care to build it up slightly in the centre to produce a gentle camber. A slope of about 1 in 30 will ensure that water drains easily from the path, so that puddles do not spoil the finish.

Step Three   Rake the gravel smooth, then roll it thoroughly with a heavy roller, watering occasionally to ensure good compaction. Once the first layer is firm, spread another layer to about the same thickness, then rake, roll and water again until compact. Be sure to maintain the camber.

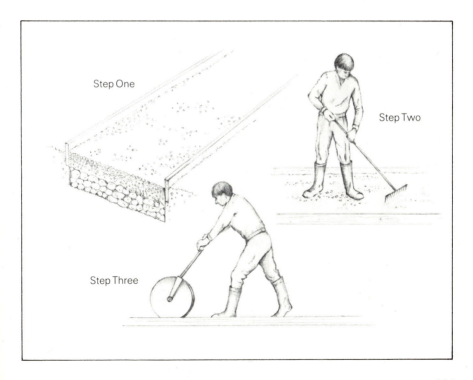

Step One

Step Two

Step Three

Laying crazy-paving

Step One   The ground should be prepared in the same way as you would for normal paving slabs (*see* page 51). Arrange the pieces roughly as you expect to use them, positioning the largest slabs first, fitting the others in like a jigsaw.

Step Two   Natural stone may be of uneven thickness, and although most of the variation can be taken up by removing or adding sand or mortar, a very thick piece may need splitting with a cold-chisel. Stand it on a bed of sand for this. A chisel can also be used to shape pieces to fit.

Step Three   When bedding in mortar, use a mix of four parts sand to one part cement. Firm the slabs well as you progress, using a straight-edged batten and spirit-level frequently to check that the paving is even.

Step Four   Finally, fill between the paving with fine soil or sand, or with the usual mix if mortar is being used. Use a damp cloth to wipe mortar off the surface. When the mortar is almost dry, but not hard, you can clean the edges with an old knife or wire brush.

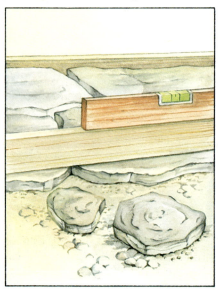 

Laying paving slabs

Step One Always lay a good foundation for paving. Excavate the ground to a sufficient depth to take about 8 cm (3 in) of consolidated hardcore, a 2.5 cm (1 in) bed of sand or mortar, and the thickness of the slab. For heavy traffic make the hardcore about 10 cm (4 in) thick and the concrete 5 cm (2 in).

Step Two For areas of light traffic, you can lay the slabs either directly on firmed sand, or use five dabs of mortar on a large slab (three on a small one). Ensure the hardcore is consolidated and levelled with ashes or sand, and use a straight-edge frequently to check levels.

Step Three Although most pre-cast paving can be bought in half-slab sizes, to even the edges, it is sometimes necessary to cut a slab to shape. Score all round the slab with a cold-chisel first, then use a bolster and heavy hammer to break the slab over a bed of sand.

Step Four Paving laid with a regular pattern is usually best pointed with mortar (one part cement to three or four parts sand) to prevent weeds becoming a problem. You can brush a dry mix between the joints, then spray lightly with water and allow it to set.

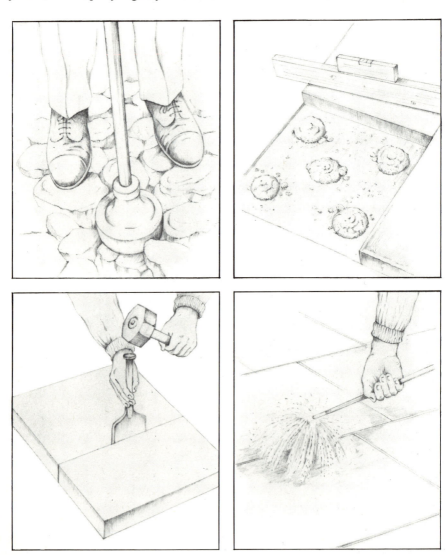

Laying a brick path

Step One Excavate the ground to take 8 cm (3 in) of compacted hardcore, 5 cm (2 in) of mortar (one part cement to three parts sharp sand), and the depth of the brick or paver. If you want to use a brick edging, lay one edge next, setting it in mortar, drawn up at the side.

Step Two Unless laying flexible paving (*see* pages 54-55), prepare a 5 cm (2 in) layer of mortar (one part cement to three parts sand), and bed the bricks in this with 6-10 mm ($\frac{1}{4}$-$\frac{1}{2}$ in) joints, using a straight-edge and spirit-level to check levels. Finally, if laying edging bricks, complete the remaining edge.

Step Three To prevent weed growth it is best to mortar between the joints. Brush dry mortar mix between the joints, making sure there are no large air pockets, then spray with water (you can use a fine-rosed watering-can). Carefully clean off any mortar on the surface of the bricks.

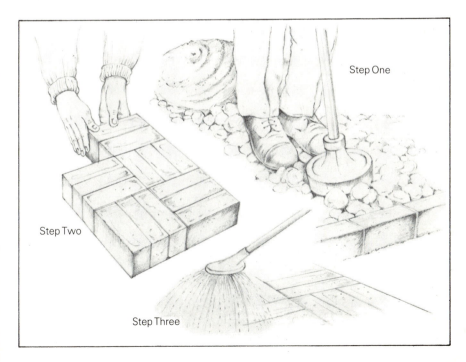

Step One

Step Two

Step Three

Interlocking concrete blocks

Step One   Remove the soil to a depth of about 11 cm (4½ in) below finished level. For a drive take out a further 10 cm (4 in) and fill with this depth of consolidated hardcore or hoggin. Finish with sand, levelling about 1.8 m (6 ft) at a time to about 4.5 cm (1¾ in) below finished level.

Step Two   Once the sand has been levelled with a board, simply place the blocks in position. Special blocks are used for the edges, but awkward areas may need blocks to be cut (you can hire a block splitter for this or use a hammer and bolster chisel).

Step Three   Once the blocks have been laid, sweep the area clean and use a hired plate vibrator to settle them in. Go over the area at least once more, then spread sand over the surface and use the vibrator again several times to settle the sand between the blocks.

Step One

Step Two

Step Three

22 Planting

The 'bricks and mortar' of construction alone will not make a garden. Such 'hard' garden features are the skeleton, on which the flesh — the plants — has to be set and shaped.

No matter how carefully you construct a pool, it will not look its best if it is not well planted (unless of course it is a formal pool where symmetry and possibly fountains hold the interest). Regardless of how carefully you shape and design your shrub border, it is of little use unless the shrubs get away to a good start, and thrive. Finally, of course, the garden hedge is just as important as a wall, and ought to receive as much care in preparation and planting.

It is with the woody plants such as trees and shrubs, that are likely to remain undisturbed for many years and normally for their lifetime (and probably for yours too in many cases), that care is especially worthwhile. No amount of trying to coax with feeds and mulches later really compensates for proper ground preparation initially.

The Soil

The soil in your garden can be an asset or a handicap, but usually there is not a lot you can do about it. You can buy in top-soil if your existing ground is really bad, but even then you are likely to remain with the underlying problem of heavy clay or perhaps chalk at the lower levels. If you do buy in soil, try to ensure that it is *good* soil, otherwise you may introduce a bigger problem than you have already. You should be able to find several sources by reading the classified advertisements in your local newspapers. A telephone call will resolve the cost and minimum load; it is usually sold by the cubic metre or yard. You can work out from this roughly how many metres or yards it will cover. If you want top-soil for a lawn, 5 cm (2 in) may be enough, for some herbaceous plants 15 cm (6 in) may be sufficient, whereas for most shrubs you will need at least 23 cm (9 in). In the case of trees you can always incorporate some good top-soil into the planting hole. Bear in mind that adding top-soil will increase the level of the beds, which you should ideally have allowed for when constructing the other features. You can always remove some of the old soil (hire a skip), but as this ought to be taken from the bottom spit, which is a major physical job, do not embark on such an exercise hastily. It is better to grow those plants that will tolerate your kind of soil, and avoid those that will not thrive. Super gardens *can* be treated on difficult soils, provided plants are chosen to suit the situation.

If you do buy fresh top-soil, try to avoid spreading it over compacted ground, so creating a distinct layer. Break up the existing soil first, and try to spread the new soil without compacting either old or new.

Whether you are managing with the existing soil or buying in new, test it before you do any planting. You can buy inexpensive kits to do this yourself, or you can send it away for analysis (you will probably have to pay for this). Certain large horticultural societies will be able to put you in touch with a suitable laboratory; otherwise contact your local parks department, who should be able to advise. The organization doing the test for you will advise on how to take and send the samples.

You may find that it is more fun to do it yourself, and the initial cost of the kits should be set off over a number of years, as you will always find a use for them on a regular basis. Lime is the easiest to test for —

There are several simple soil-testing kits that you can buy. A sample of soil is taken from various parts of the garden, and a measured amount is mixed with an indicator fluid and the colour compared against a chart.

or more precisely the pH; this test, in simple terms, tells you how limy (alkaline) or acid it is. In many ways this is one of the most useful tests. The kit will tell you how much lime to put on to bring the soil up to the required level (although the ideal level depends on the plants). If it is already too alkaline (limy) you can apply aluminium sulphate or sulphate of ammonia (but aluminium sulphate is poisonous and should not be used on food crops, and sulphate of ammonia is a fertilizer and can be overdone); again the kit should advise on this. If the soil is very acid, or very alkaline, it is probably best to adjust your choice of plants rather than attempt to change the soil. If you simply must grow some plants that will not be happy, treat the soil in just one bed, grow in containers, or try to treat the soil just in the area of your special plants.

If you want to grow an acid-loving plant in a chalky garden, you can try making a large polythene-lined planting pocket.

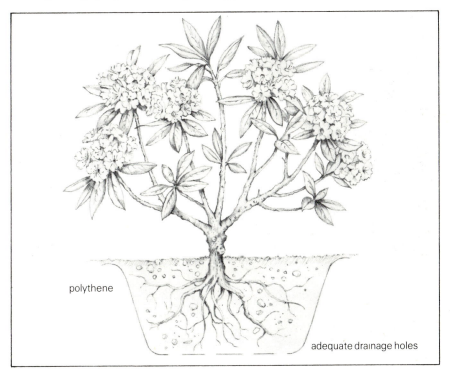

polythene

adequate drainage holes

Some soil-testing kits will tell you whether your soil is deficient in the major plant nutrients, which are nitrogen, phosphates and potash. Unfortunately these are not as easy and reliable to test for outside the laboratory, but they are better than having no idea of nutrient deficiencies.

It is always worth applying a general fertilizer anyway, either a week or two before planting or in spring if planting takes place in winter, but the soil test will tell you whether your soil needs an extra dose of any particular nutrient.

Take the opportunity to dig the ground thoroughly before planting, breaking up the bottom spit (spade depth) if possible. If the area is large it may be worth hiring a rotary cultivator. This is not always a good idea; if you have a lot of perennial weeds with fleshy roots or underground stolons, there is a danger that they will simply be chopped up and you will have more difficult weeds than you started with. Fortunately there are useful weedkillers, such as glyphosate, that will probably kill these weeds and yet still leave the soil ready for

A 'spit' is the depth of the spade blade.

Double digging, adding compost to the bottom spit.

Camellias do quite well in tubs or other large containers, and are worth trying this way if you have an alkaline soil.

planting. Weedkillers and rotary cultivators are worth considering if you are unable to tackle the physically hard work of cleaning the land by hand.

While cultivating the soil, it is also worth taking the opportunity to incorporate plenty of organic matter, as practically all soils will benefit. Unfortunately few of us generate sufficient garden compost to go very far, and peat is extremely expensive to use in the quantities required. Sometimes, however, it is possible to find a local supply of bulky organic material such as spent hops or spent mushroom compost (remember this contains chalk).

If you just cannot find enough to go round the garden in sufficient quantity, save it for the planting holes, rather than spread it around too thinly.

The Plants

Buy plants with as much care as you would other materials. Quality *is* important. A well-grown plant in good health that has not received a check could easily grow away quickly and save you a year's growth over a poorer specimen of the same age and size when planted.

In some cases the actual quality of flowers or fruit may be superior from a nursery selling a good strain or disease-free stock.

You can end up with good or poor quality whether you buy from a nursery, garden centre, or by mail order. If buying personally from a nursery or garden centre, you can assess the stock first and it is only your own fault if you buy poor quality.

If you are shopping by mail order, the reputation of the company is your main guide. You can often gauge from their catalogue the type of nursery they are, and probable quality of stock. The mail order companies to be more cautious of are those advertising bargain offers in newspapers. You may get a good buy (sometimes the plants may be small but satisfactory), but you are less likely to obtain first-class plants.

The hints on pages 123–5 will tell you what to look for.

When to Plant

Container-grown plants can be planted at any time, provided the soil is not frozen or waterlogged. Bare-root and 'balled' plants should be planted at the following times.

Deciduous trees and shrubs, including roses, are best planted from the end of October to the beginning of April.

Evergreens, including conifers, are best planted in September/ October or March/April.

Herbaceous perennials can be planted from September to the end of April.

Water-lilies and marginal aquatics are normally planted in April, May or early June.

How Far Apart to Plant

It is not easy to know how much space to leave between plants; so much depends on your patience and characteristics of the particular plant.

Herbaceous plants are the easiest to estimate as they reach their ultimate height within a couple of seasons, and their vigour and

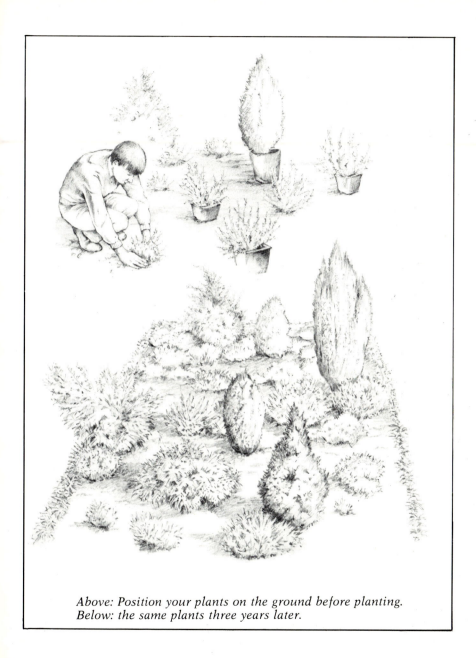

Above: Position your plants on the ground before planting.
Below: the same plants three years later.

spread is easily gauged. As a very approximate guide, 30-45 cm (1-1½ ft) is about right for average kinds, while vigorous ones will need, say, 60-90 cm (2-3 ft) spacing. Nevertheless, go by your assessment of the individual plant. You may need to move border plants around anyway because herbaceous borders planned on paper do not always work out first time in reality.

Ground cover plants vary considerably in vigour. Some are quite compact whereas others are rampant. The rampant ones can be spaced quite far apart. However, as most of us are impatient for ground cover to do its work, 20-30 cm (8-12 in) is about right for most of them, if you do not have any more precise guidance. This may be close for vigorous kinds, but these are usually relatively cheap anyway, and will help to achieve cover more quickly.

The real difficulty comes with trees and shrubs. If you plant at the right spacings for say 15 years of growth, you are likely to have a bare garden in the meantime. The solution is to plant more shrubs than you will need in the long term, being prepared to thin out once they become too large; or use border plants or large, gap-filling annuals to clothe the area for the first few years. In the case of trees it is usually possible to position these by taking the probable height in say 15-20 years (especially if you avoid the large, forest trees). Good books will give you the probable height at this time. As a rough guide, dwarf and slow-growing shrubs should be planted 45-60 cm (1½-2 ft) apart, those of medium ultimate size, 90 cm-1.2 m (3-4 ft) and vigorous kinds 1.5-1.8 m (5-6 ft) apart.

Left: Always try to plant a tree or shrub at the depth it was growing before.

Top right: Remove the container before planting. Most can be cut with scissors or slit with a knife.

Top far right: Add damp peat to the planting hole and mix it in. Tease out a few roots from the root-ball.

Right: Firm the plant well by treading the soil round the plant with the heel.

Far right: Unless it is wet, always water thoroughly.

114

Materials

Paving and Walling Blocks

Most garden centres have a range of paving, but you may find a wider selection at a good builders' merchant. Manufacturers usually provide informative, illustrated brochures (which are particularly useful at the planning stage) but distribution is usually through garden centres and builders' merchants. If you want a particular product the manufacturer will always give you the address of the nearest stockist. It is also worth looking in the local newspaper advertisements.

You may have to pay a delivery charge, so buying from a builders' merchant will probably mean that it makes sense to have sand, cement and any other materials delivered at the same time. It is wise to allow up to 5 per cent for breakages.

Paving slabs and blocks are frequently sold individually, but sometimes they will be sold by the square metre. It is simple to work out the number of rectangular blocks. If you are using various colours and sizes, draw the pattern on graph paper then count how many of each kind you will need; but some angled concrete paving blocks are more difficult to estimate, especially because of the special edge and end blocks that are needed. In these cases the manufacturer will provide the formula for working out how many you need, or your supplier will work it out for you. The vital measurements are total area (length × breadth), the linear metres of ends, and linear metres of edges (sides).

Bricks

Here you have little choice but to go to a good builders' merchant. Even then he can only hold stock of a limited range, although it should be perfectly possible to find a suitable type for what you want.

The vital thing to remember is that they must be suitable for exposure to soaking and freezing. Most 'special quality' bricks meet

You can buy large specimen trees, though they are usually very expensive. Younger plants are often a better buy.

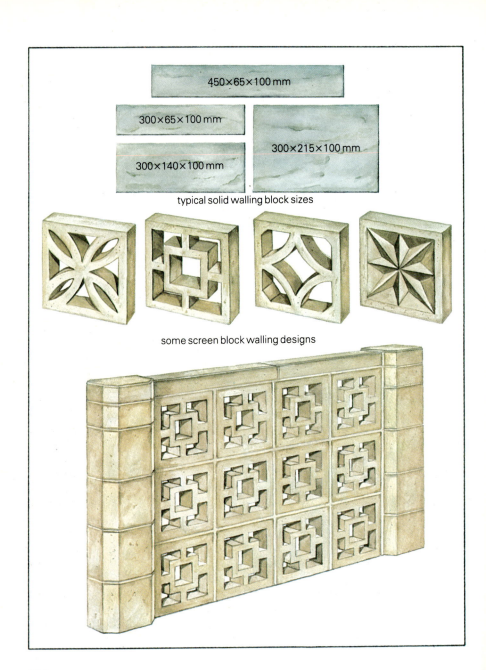

450×65×100 mm

300×65×100 mm

300×215×100 mm

300×140×100 mm

typical solid walling block sizes

some screen block walling designs

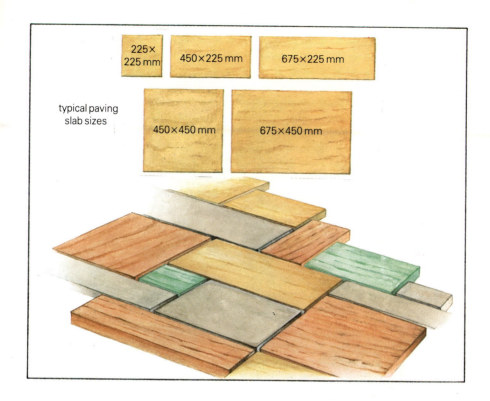

typical paving slab sizes

225 × 225 mm
450 × 225 mm
675 × 225 mm
450 × 450 mm
675 × 450 mm

this requirement. Soft facing bricks that might be quite suitable for housing are usually unsuitable for paving or garden walls (which are exposed to the weather on both sides).

Most bricks are of a standard size: 215 mm long, 102 mm wide, and 65 mm deep; allowing a nominal 10 mm for joints, you can calculate on the basis of $225 \times 112 \times 75$ mm (say $8\frac{7}{8} \times 4\frac{3}{8} \times 3$ in). For a wall a single brick wide (technically a 'half brick' wall) you will need 60 bricks for each square metre, 120 bricks for a wall two bricks wide (technically a 'full brick' wall).

It is best to avoid bricks with a very smooth surface, as they may become too slippery when wet.

Clay pavers are specially designed for paving; they are thinner than normal bricks, and because no allowance is made for mortar with 'flexible' pavers they fit together better than ordinary bricks would if laid 'dry'. Dimensions may vary from product to product, so always check this.

Concrete Mixes

You can buy concrete ready-mixed, but you are likely to have to take a minimum load of about 3 m³ (about 7½ tons), which you will have to lay within a couple of hours! For a large area, and if you have help available, it is worth considering. Of course it is only a practical proposition if the lorry has suitable access to the site.

Dry-batched (sometimes called dry-mix) concrete or mortar is bought with the ingredients ready mixed, and you only have to add water. For a very small job, where one or two bags will be enough, this is the most convenient. Even on jobs taking perhaps five bags you may be prepared to pay for the convenience. If ten or more would be needed it makes most sense to buy the separate ingredients and mix your own. Dry-mix concrete or mortar has the advantage of coming in easily handled bags (even if heavy) which means that you can bring it home in the car. Loose sand and gravel has to be delivered (unless you have a truck), and they may not be keen on delivering less than say 0.5 tonne.

Cement is normally ordinary Portland cement (this is a type, not a brand). The sand you should use for concrete is concreting or sharp sand. Gravel tends to vary, usually between 5 mm ($\frac{3}{16}$ in) and 20 mm ($\frac{3}{4}$ in) across. Standard sizes are 20–10 mm, 20–5 mm, 10–5 mm, and 20 mm down.

Likely Amount of Concrete or Ingredients Needed For 10 m² (100 sq ft)

Thickness of concrete	Ready mixed	Dry mix (50 kg/1 cwt bags)	1:2:3 concrete mix	
			Cement (50 kg/1 cwt bags)	Combined aggregate
50 mm (2 in)	0.5 m³	22 bags	4 bags	0.5 m³
75 mm (3 in)	0.75 m³	33 bags	6 bags	0.75 m³
100 mm (4 in)	1 m³	44 bags	7 bags	1 m³

NOTE: For the quantities given, dry mix would be expensive. If you do want to use this it is best to get it delivered rather than make repeated journeys in the car. The amount of cement is given rounded up to the next full bag. Treat these figures only as a guide.

It is convenient to buy the sand and gravel already mixed, when it is called combined or all-in aggregate (also referred to as ballast), but it is a frequent cause of failure. Poor grading can lead to a weak mix susceptible to frost damage.

Mortar Mixes

For mortar you need a different sand, usually described as soft or building sand. You can use ordinary Portland cement, but to make the mortar more workable without adding so much water that quality is reduced, you can add a plasticizer. The cement sold as masonry cement already has a plasticizer added.

Gravel

Gravel is a variable material, much depending on the source of supply. Local gravels are naturally cheapest. For paths, washed pea gravel, from gravel pits and river beds, is suitable. It may be available in various shades of brown. As a guide, 1 tonne (1 ton) of pea gravel will cover about 10 m² (100 sq ft) to a depth of about 7.5 cm (3 in).

Hardcore

Hardcore is of very variable quality. Sometimes it consists of large building rubble difficult to break down into pieces small enough to compact for a shallow foundation. For most purposes a graded 2.5 cm (1 in) maximum sized stone is adequate. You may be able to buy this from a builders' merchant, otherwise you will have to contact a quarry. It is best to see what you are buying.

Rockery Stone

Rockery stone is a variable product to buy, and it is sometimes difficult to estimate the quantity required.

A local sandstone might contain perhaps 30 pieces and weigh just over a tonne (ton), whereas individual large pieces will weigh more than 50 kg (1 cwt).

It is best to see the rocks first as different types vary significantly in appearance and size. As an approximate guide a cubic yard of sandstone might be enough for 4 m² (5 sq yd) of rockery.

One company's ½ cubic yard of grit — more in reality!

This is 1 cubic yard of pea shingle.

Buying Wood

Unless you are making a greenhouse, or something of similar importance, common deal or softwood is probably going to be adequate (provided that it is treated where necessary). There is no such tree as deal, and the term is used loosely to cover softwoods such as redwood and whitewood. In the case of fencing posts, it is usually best to buy timber sold for this and supplied by a fencing supplier, who will probably have had it impregnated with a suitable preservative.

For a garden seat you can choose between a hardwood like iroko, which is robust and not too expensive, and contains a natural preservative, or a softwood such as Douglas fir. With a softwood you will have to use a preservative regularly.

Rough or sawn timber may be perfectly suitable for many outdoor jobs (a timber-framed pergola, for instance) but for the framework of a cold-frame, for example, planed wood is required. Bear in mind that planed wood is smaller than the nominal size stated. As a guide, timber with a dimension up to 100 mm is likely to lose 4 mm, whereas larger sizes will probably lose 6 mm.

As wood is sold in metric measurements, it pays to measure up in metric; otherwise you will be sold the next metric size up, and you may pay for more than you need. Lengths normally start at 1.8 m (about 6 ft), and go in steps of 300 mm (just under 1 ft): 1.8 m, 2.1 m, 2.4 m and so on. The nominal sizes remain the same as the old imperial, but expressed in millimetres: 1 in = 25 mm, 2 in = 50 mm, 3 in = 75 mm, and so on.

Buying Plants

Because plants are living things, it is much more difficult to be sure that you are buying the best. Sometimes you are buying what looks like little more than a cluster of dead twigs in the dormant season. Even if you purchase a container-grown plant in the summer, there is often little guarantee that the plant is true to name, or a good strain.

For these reasons it makes sense to buy your plants from a reputable nursery or garden centre.

Rock plants Most rock garden or alpine plants are sold in pots (though obviously mail-order plants are likely to be removed from the actual pot). Look for plants that seem well established in their pots, but avoid any that are obviously pot-bound. Do not buy if the plants have obviously been allowed to dry out. A clear label is a good sign.

Border plants Strain can be important here; some may be seed-raised forms that are often inferior to those raised by cuttings from good stock. It is not always possible to tell, of course, but if the full plant name is given, and the name of the nursery is a very reputable one, you are fairly safe. You can purchase container-grown plants, but in the spring you can usually buy plants with their roots wrapped in damp peat and moss. These are cheaper and often just as good, provided that they are not too advanced into growth.

Trees and shrubs There is usually a choice between 'balled' plants, bare-root plants, and those grown in containers. 'Balled' plants have the root-ball wrapped in a hessian or plastic mesh, or sometimes polythene. Conifers are frequently sold this way. There is obviously more root disturbance than with a container-grown plant, but less than there would be if all the soil had been removed. Only buy balled specimens that have been kept in damp peat or soil, and ensure that the soil-ball is large and firm. Plastic materials must be removed before planting.

Bare-root plants are generally cheaper than container-grown specimens. Such trees and shrubs (including roses) will usually establish perfectly satisfactorily, provided that they are not allowed to dry out, and are planted in the dormant season. Beware of bare-root shrubs packed in polythene sleeves if they are lightweight or have shrivelled stems. Likewise avoid any with diseased or very pale leaves or shoots.

Container-grown plants have the advantage of least root disturbance, and can be planted at any time; but ensure that they have not only recently been planted in the container. You should be able to lift the plant up by the stem without it coming loose. A little mossy growth, or even some weed seedlings, on the surface indicates a plant that should be well rooted in the compost. Avoid any where there is a lot of root growth through the base of the pot (although a little is perfectly acceptable).

A few roots growing through the container can be a good sign, provided there are not too many.

A sign of well cared for plants: trees well supported, automatic watering, adequate containers, and good labelling.

Hedging plants Generally, strong young plants will grow away and quickly catch up larger plants, and they will be cheaper. Do not buy bare-root hedges if there is any suggestion that the roots could have dried out. Conifers for hedging are usually pot-grown, and it is worth paying the little extra for this as they are expensive plants to lose.

Index

Figures in italics refer to page numbers of illustrations.